Vision Board & Clip Art Book for Black Women:
Empower & Achieve

Abyy Sparklewood
Copyright © 2024 All rights reserved.
978-1-961634-54-1

Welcome to "Empower: Your Vision Board and Clip Art Book for Black Women"!

This book is your creative playground, filled with:
- Inspiring images
- Affirmations
- Empowering quotes

Designed to help you:
- Manifest your dreams
- Embrace your fullest potential

Whether you envision financial freedom, career success, or personal growth, this book is your companion on the journey to greatness.

Dive into pages brimming with:
- Vibrant clip art
- Symbols of wealth and abundance
- Uplifting portraits of powerful Black women

Let your imagination soar as you craft a vision board that reflects your unique aspirations and celebrates your beautiful, unstoppable self.

Get ready to:
- Turn your dreams into reality
- Empower yourself
- Prosper

Your journey to empowerment and prosperity starts here!

Introduction:

Welcome to the world of vision boards! Imagine having a powerful tool that can help you visualize your dreams, set clear goals, and manifest your deepest desires. That's exactly what a vision board is all about.

A vision board is a visual representation of your goals and aspirations. It's a collage of images, words, and affirmations that resonate with your ambitions, serving as a daily reminder of where you want to go and what you want to achieve.

Why are vision boards important? They are a constant source of motivation and inspiration, helping you stay focused on your goals. Seeing your dreams laid out visually reinforces your commitment and drives you to take actionable steps toward making them a reality. Vision boards tap into the power of visualization, a technique successful people use to attract positive outcomes and achieve their goals.

In this clip art book, you'll find a variety of creative and inspiring images to help you craft your vision board. Whether you're aiming for personal growth, career success, health and wellness, or financial abundance, these clip arts will bring your dreams to life. Get ready to embark on a journey of self-discovery and empowerment as you create a vision board that truly reflects your aspirations. Let's turn those dreams into reality, one image at a time!

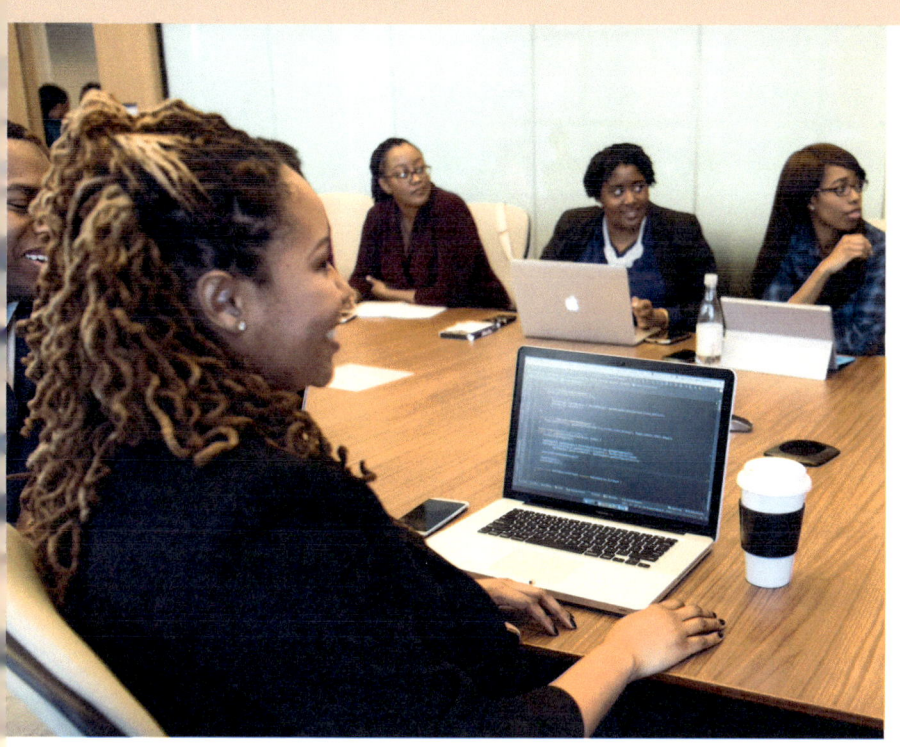
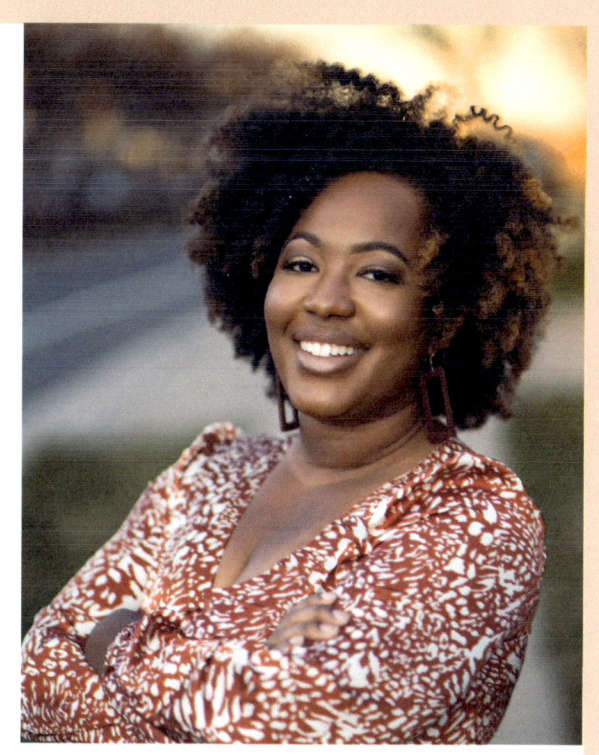
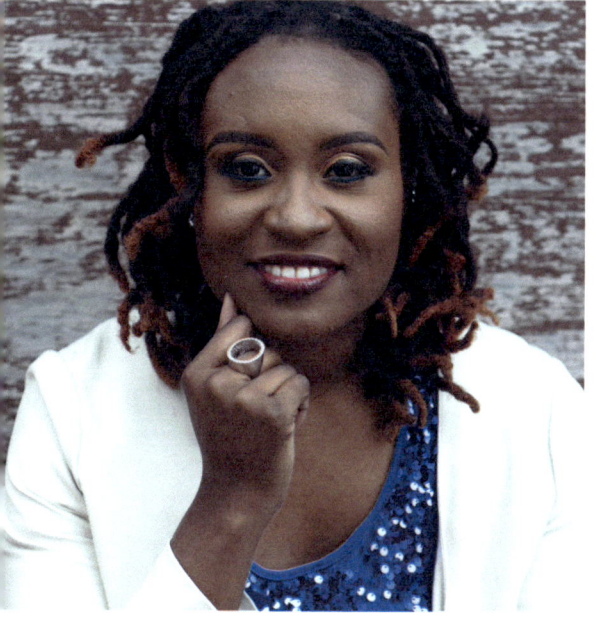
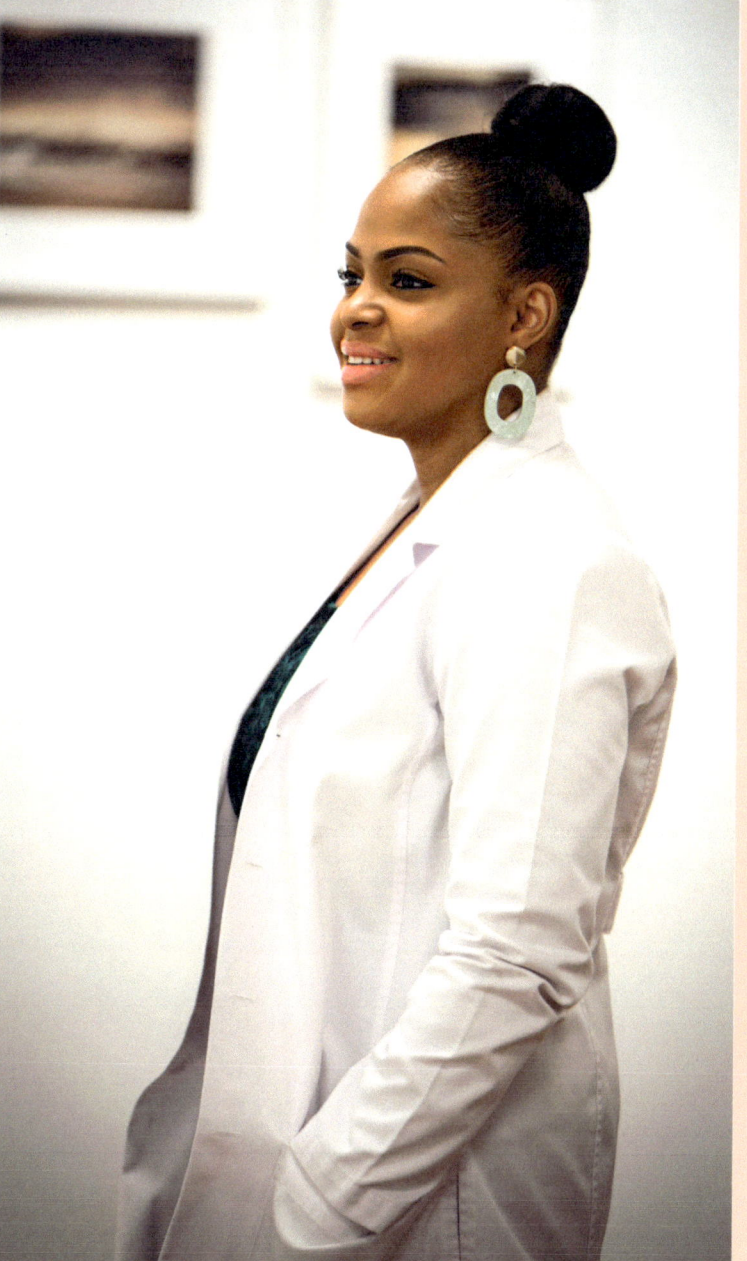

career

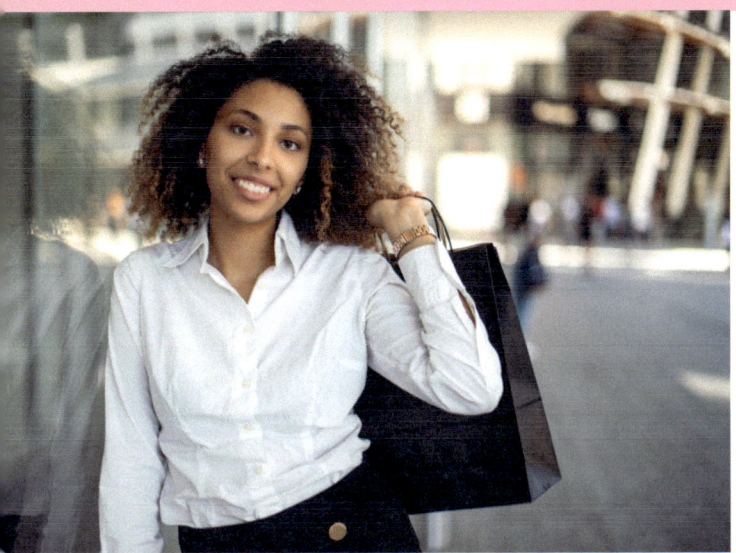
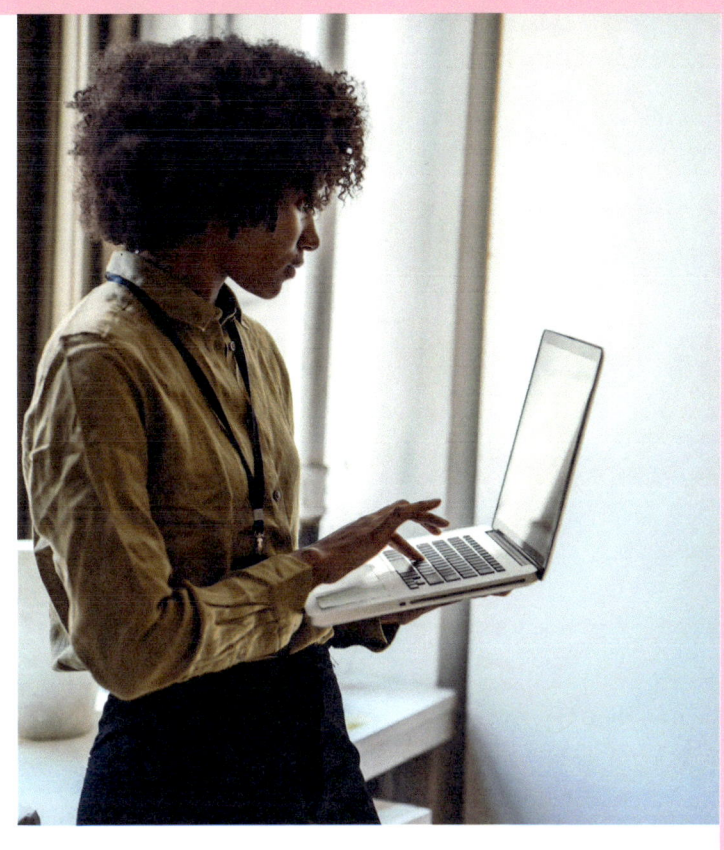
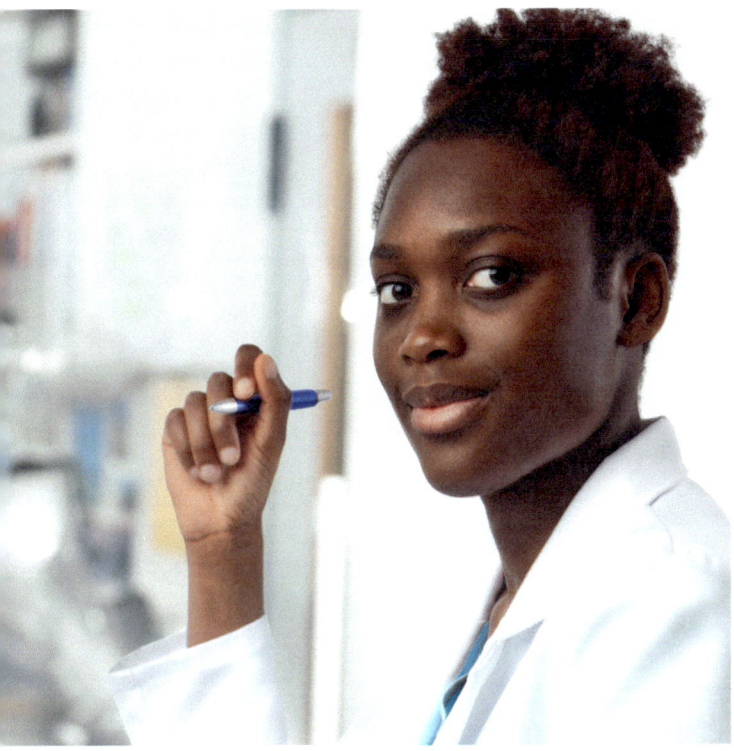

SUCCESS IS NOT JUST ABOUT REACHING THE TOP; IT'S ABOUT BRINGING OTHERS UP WITH YOU. LIFT AS YOU CLIMB, FEMALE ENTREPRENEURS

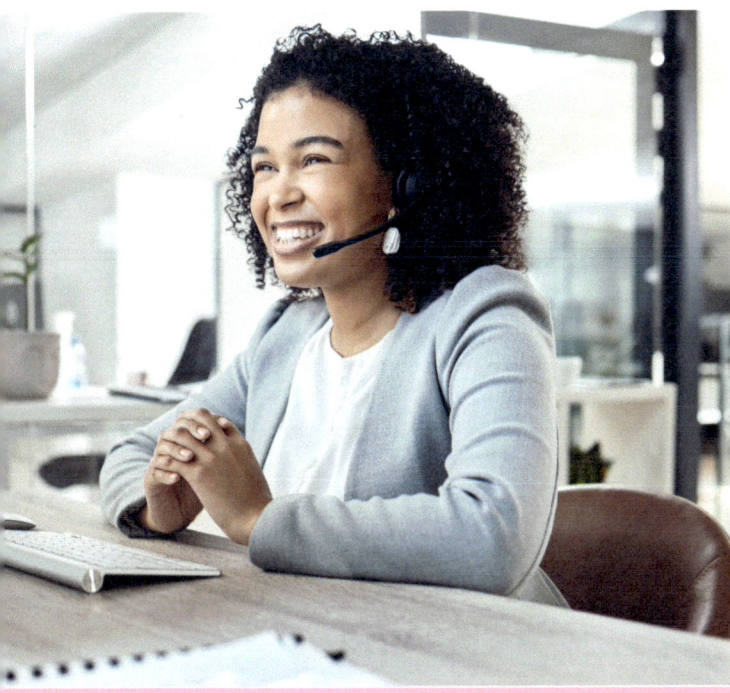
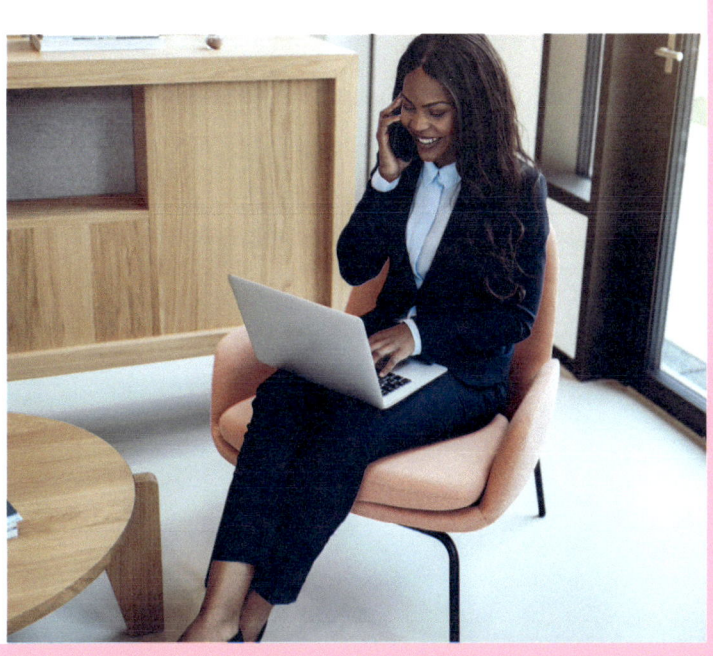

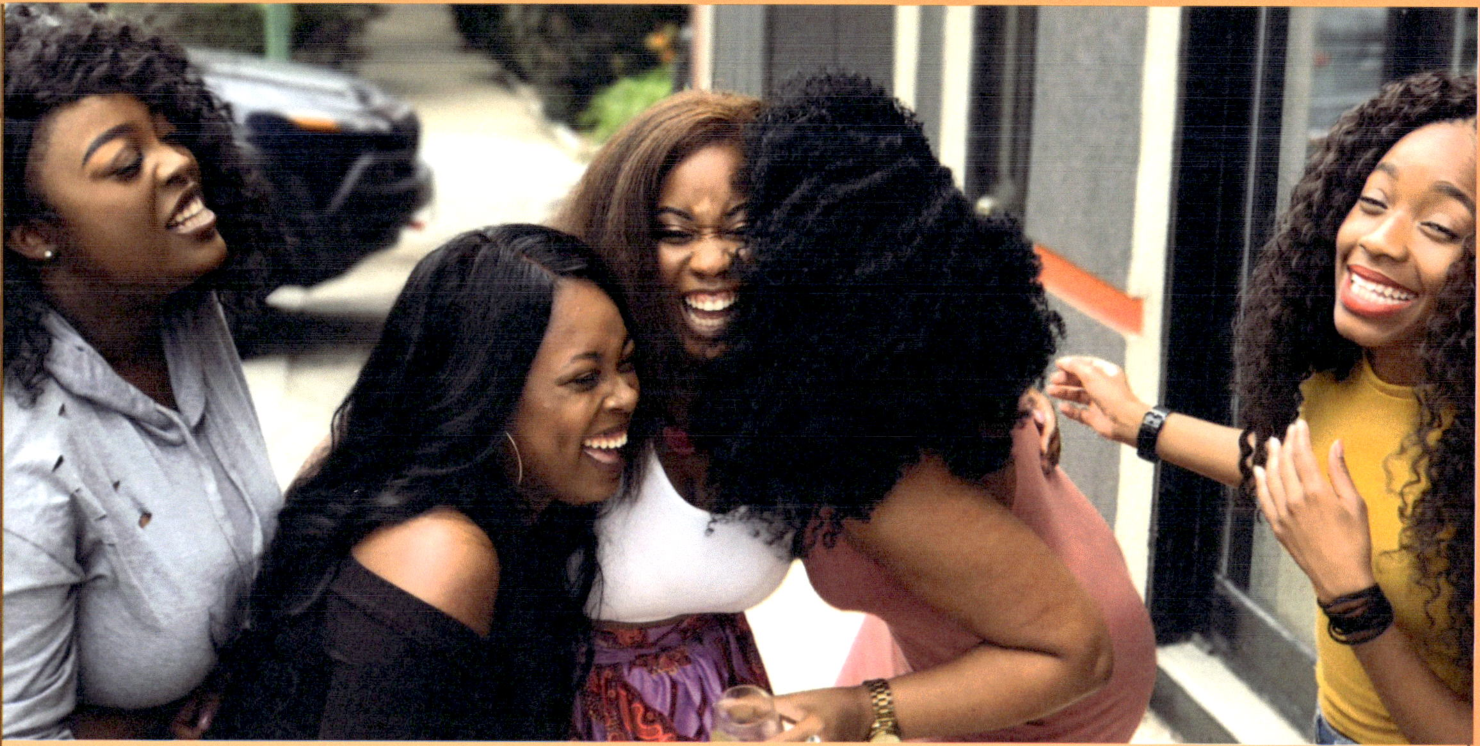

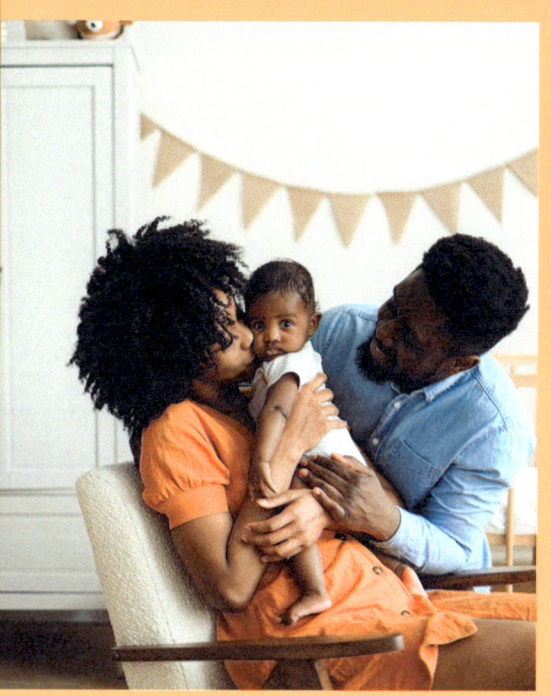
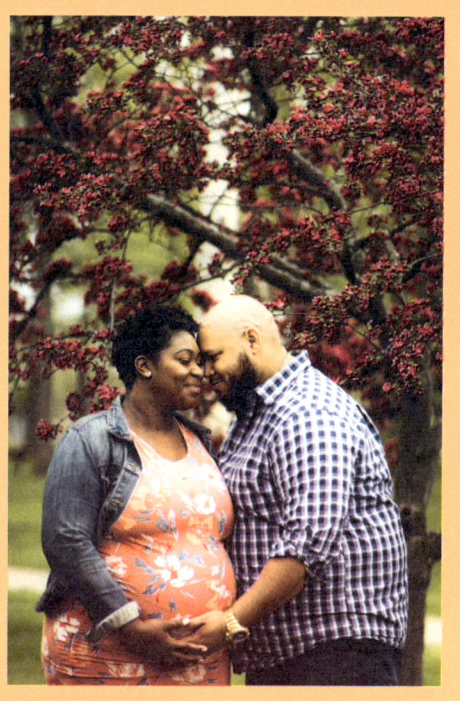

Love, family, Unity, Forever

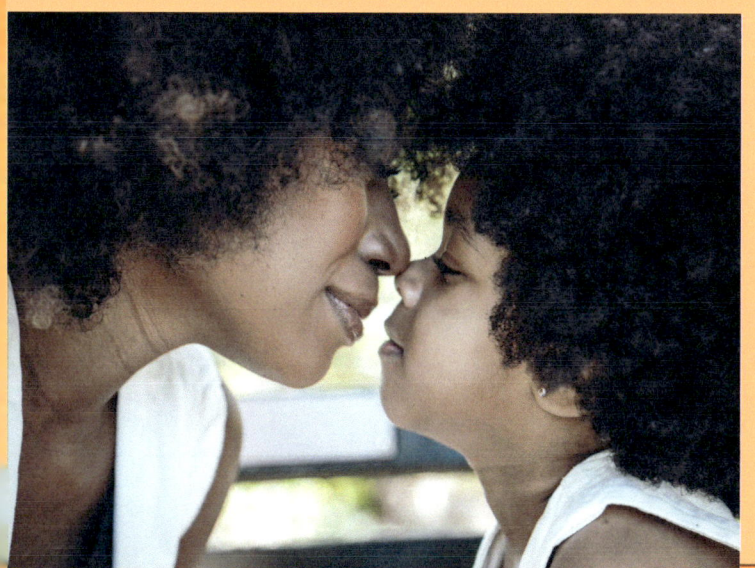
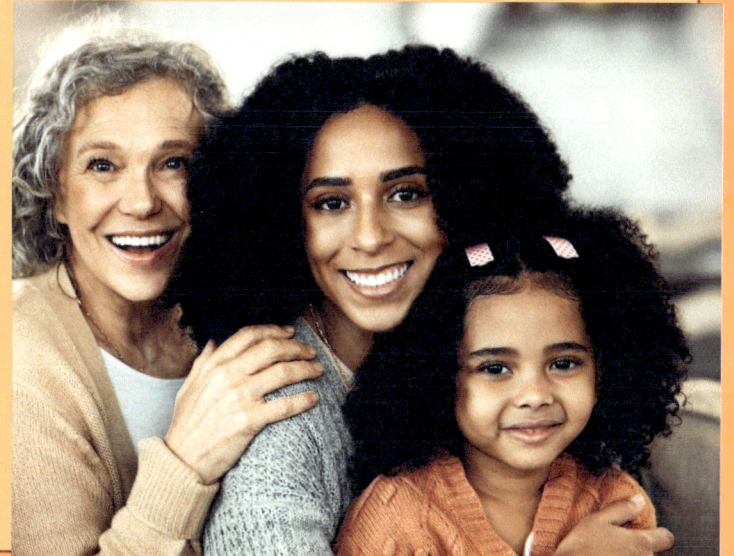

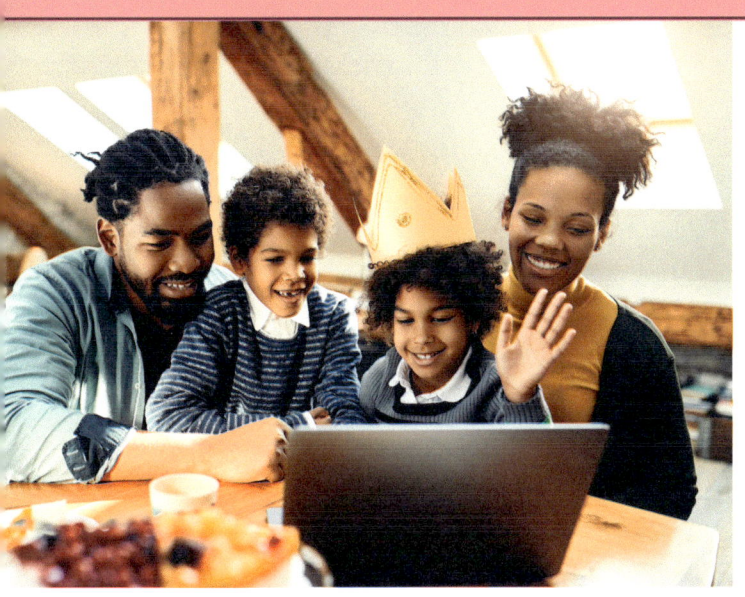
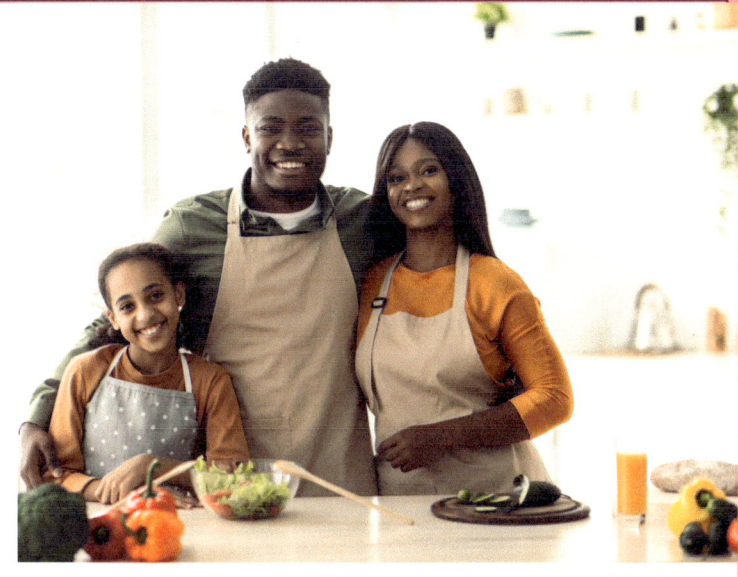

"I nurture and uplift my family with love, strength, and unwavering support."

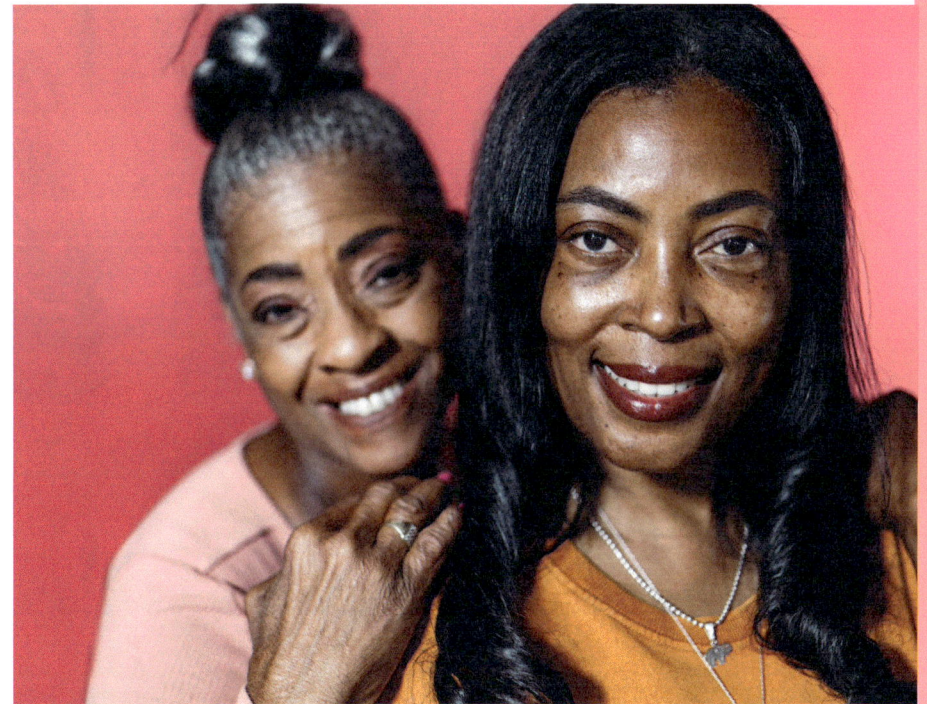
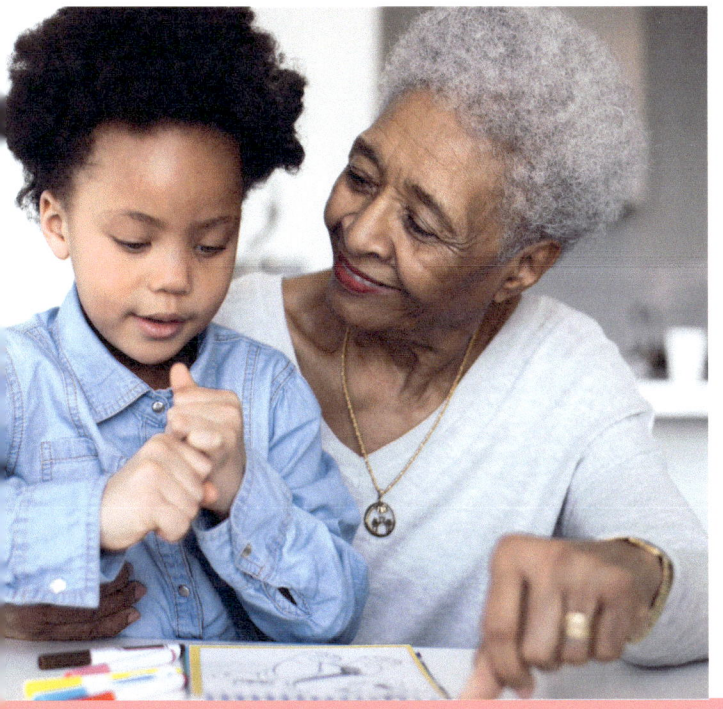
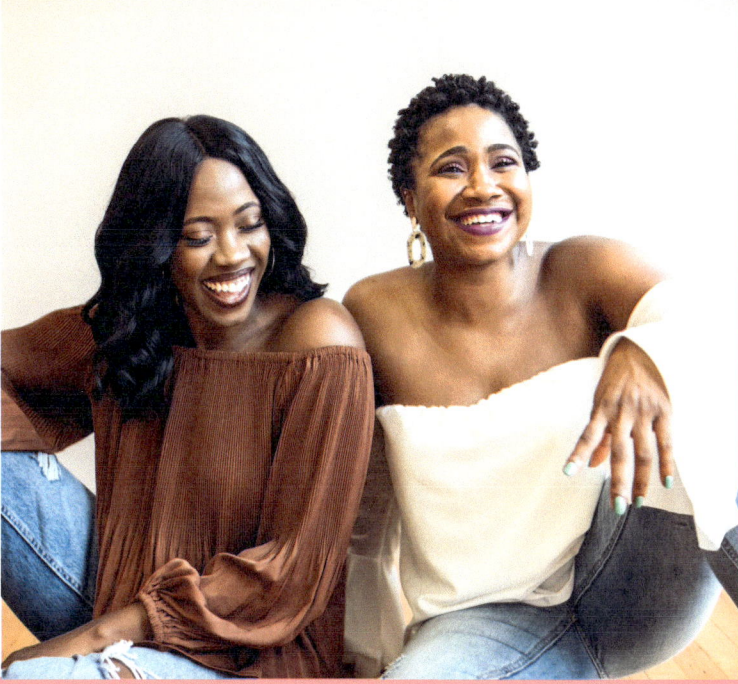

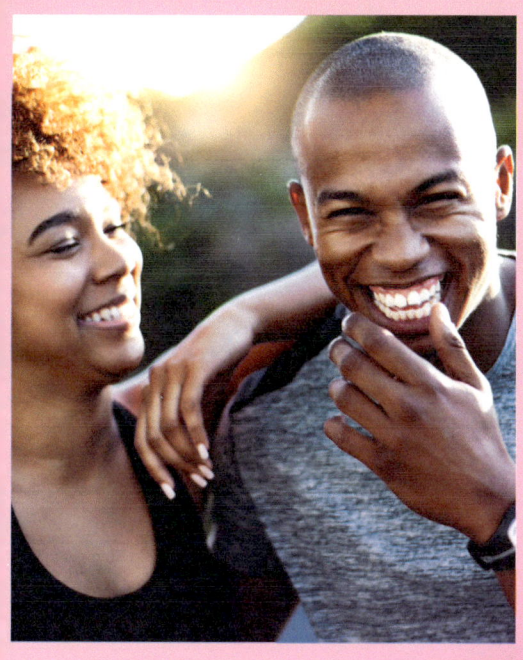
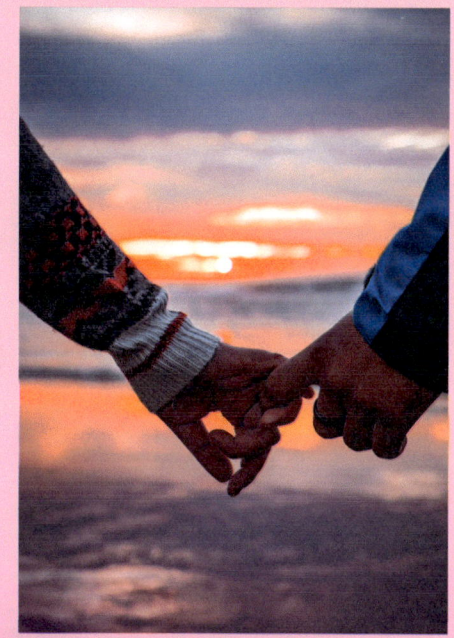
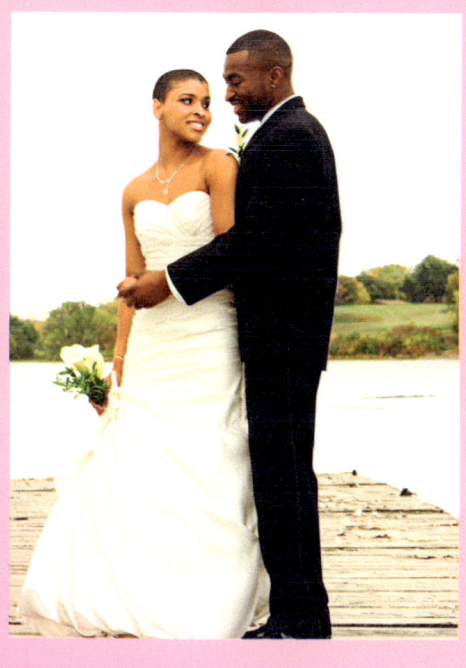

love
AND MARRIAGE!

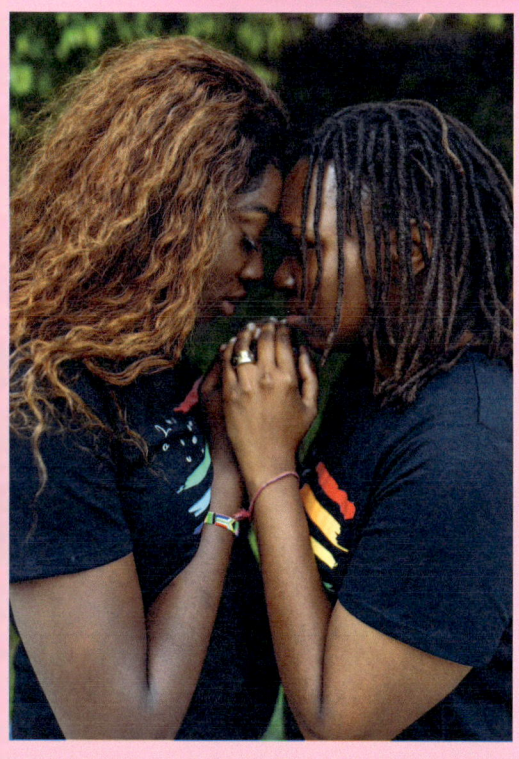
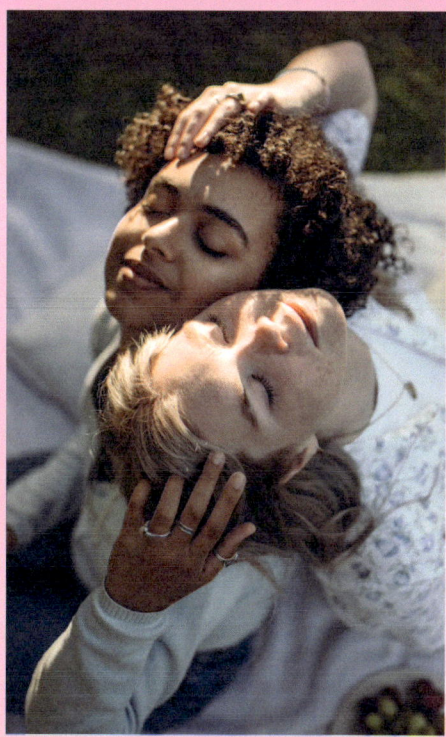
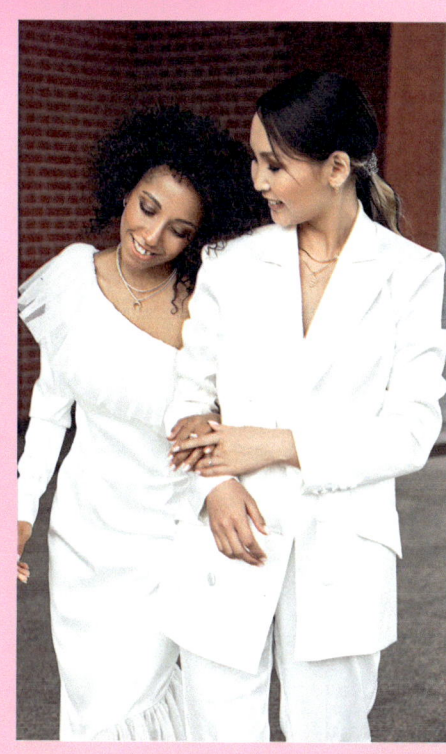

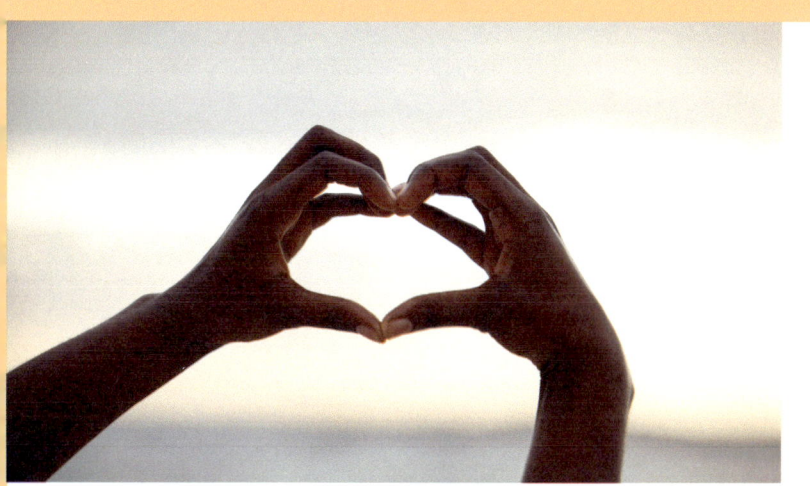
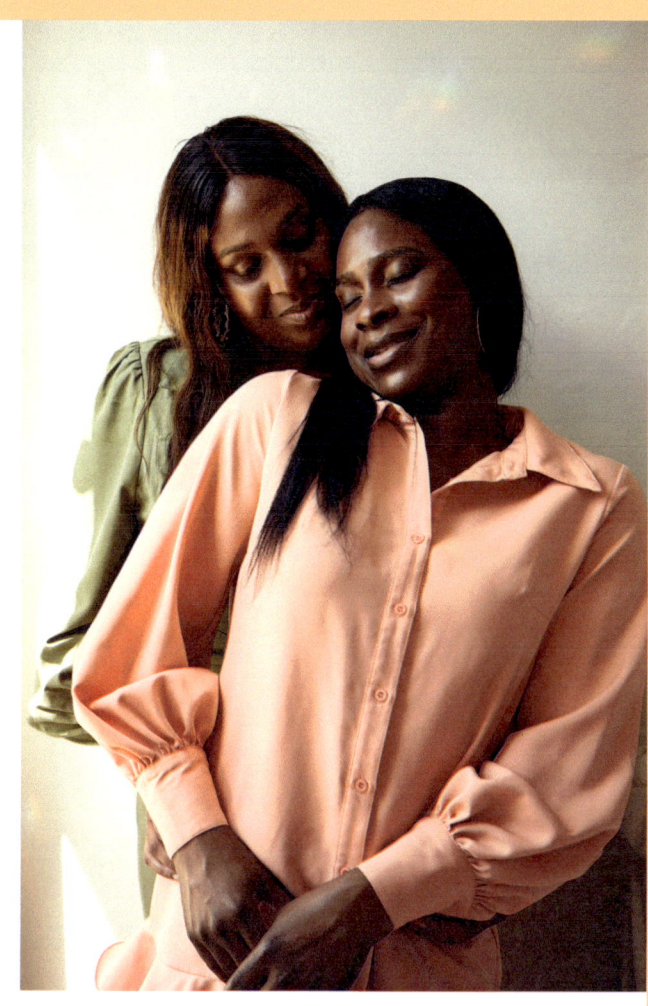
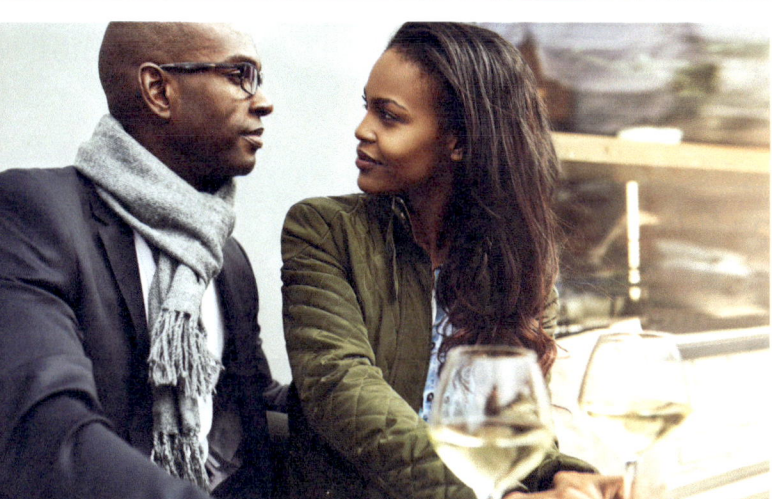

Yes I am worthy of love

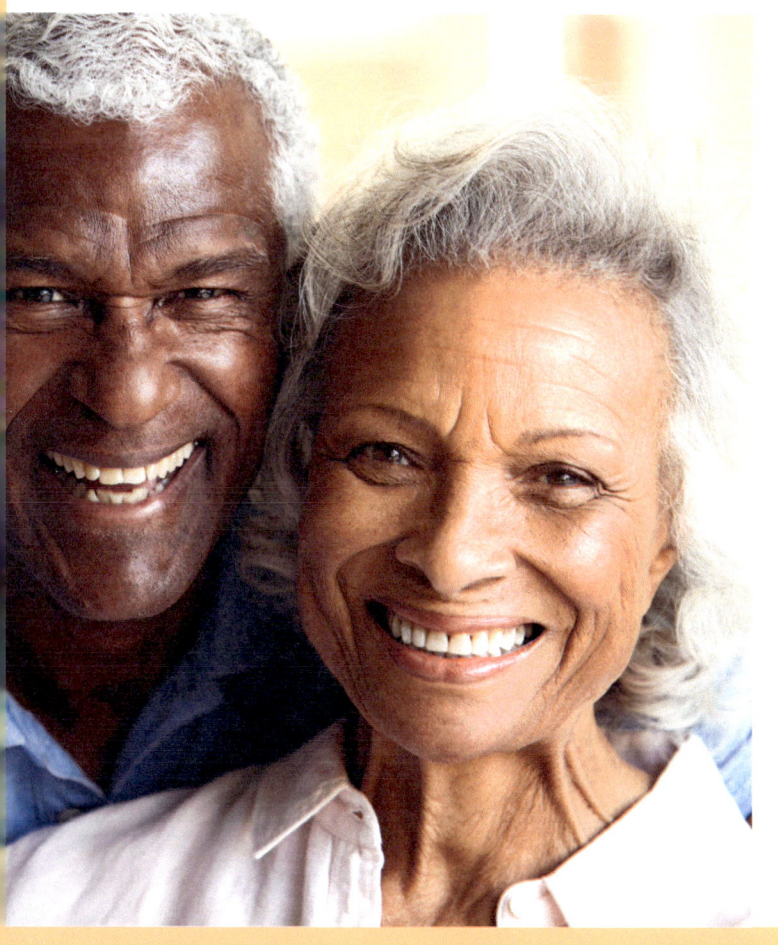
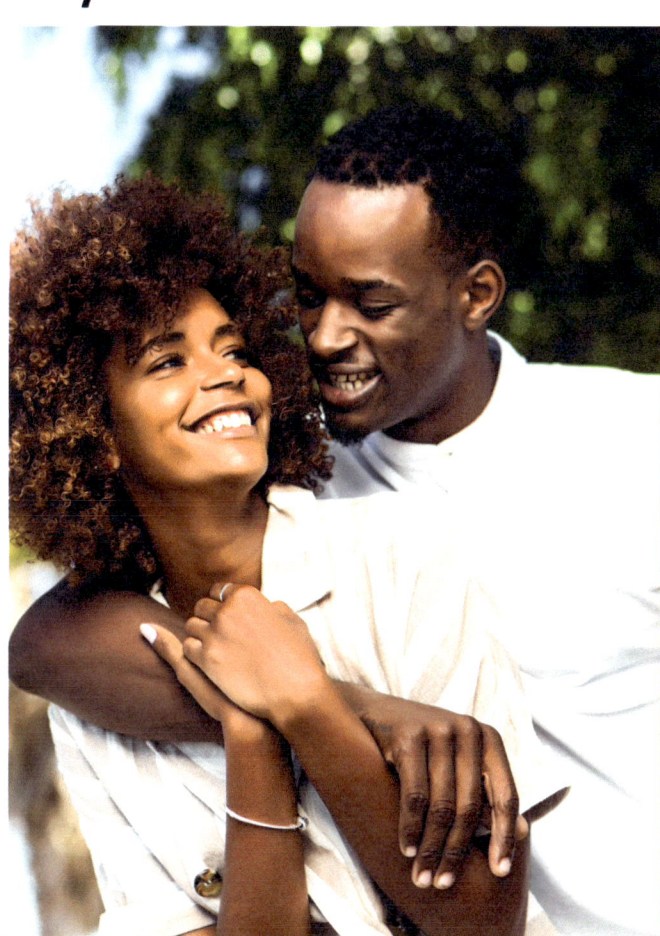

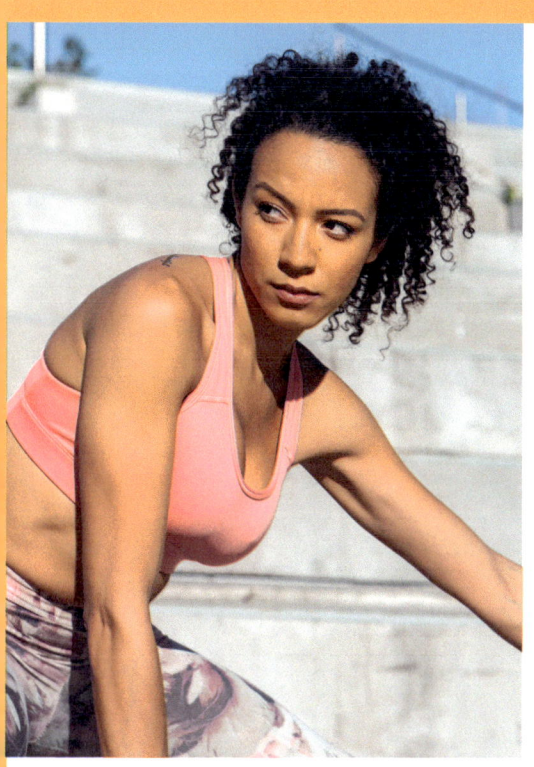
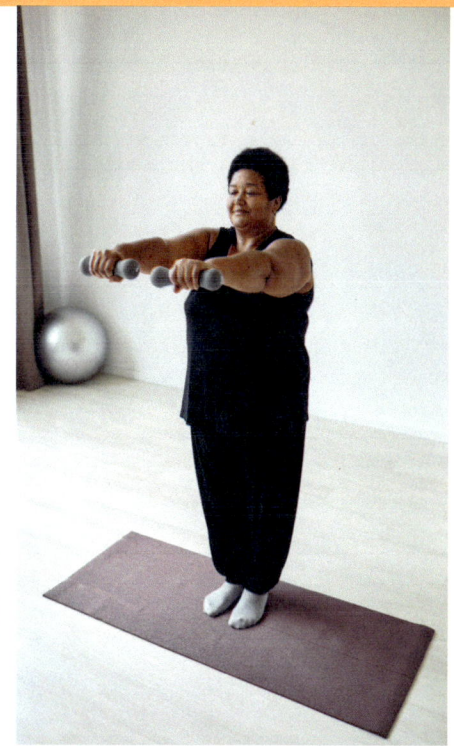
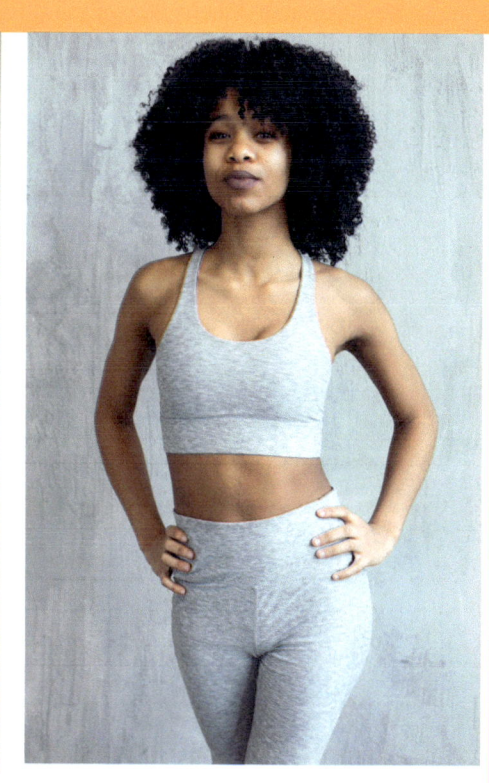
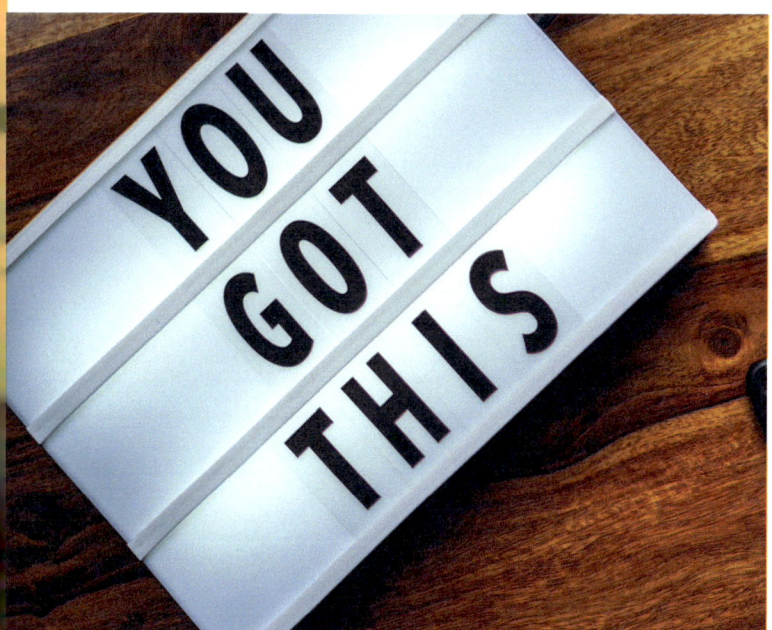
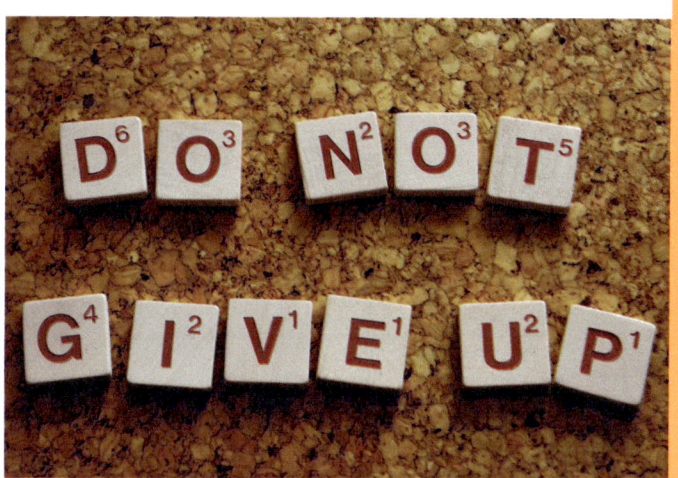

Fitness & Excercise

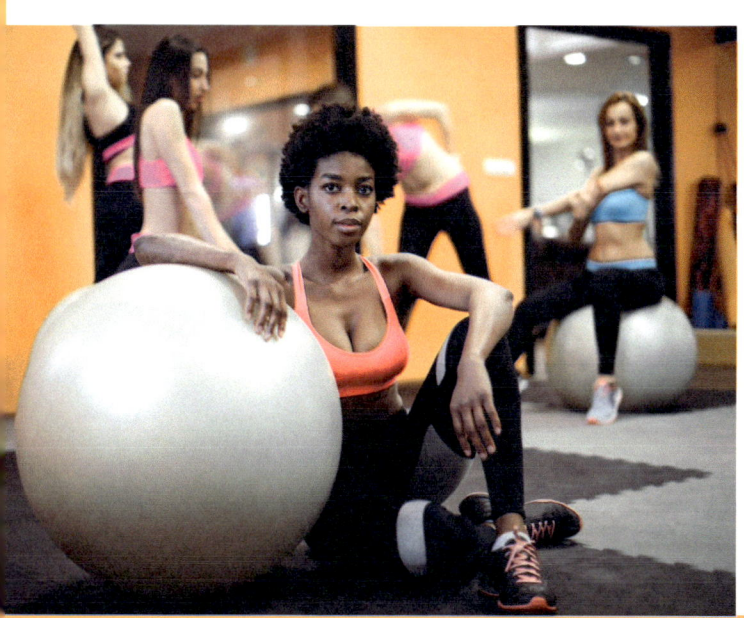
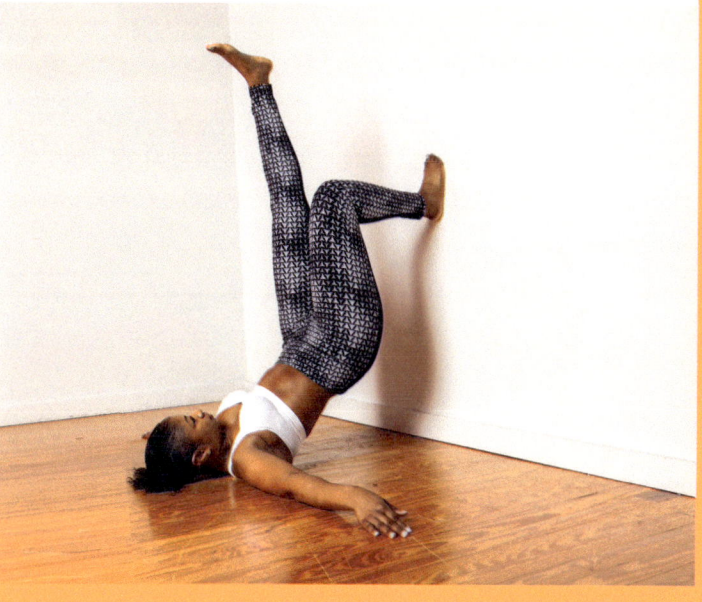

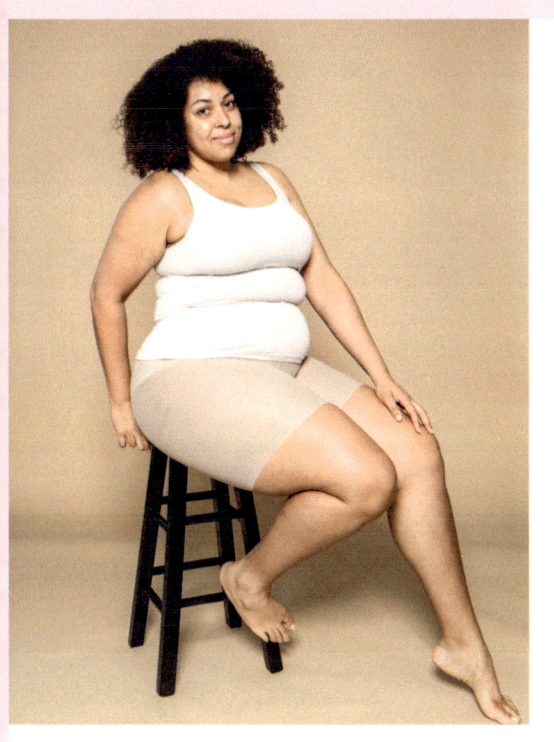
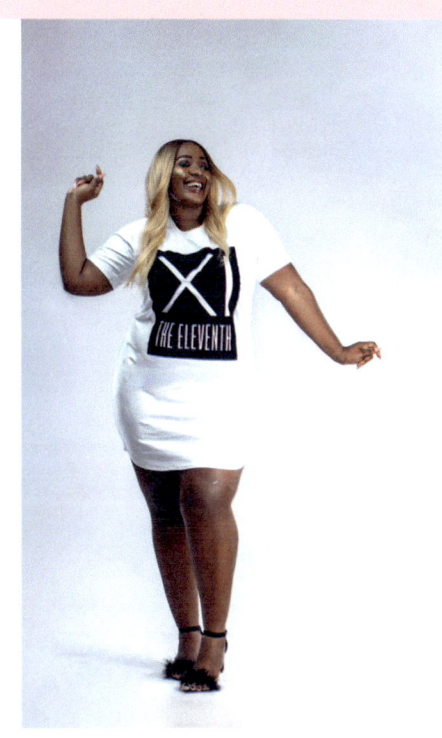
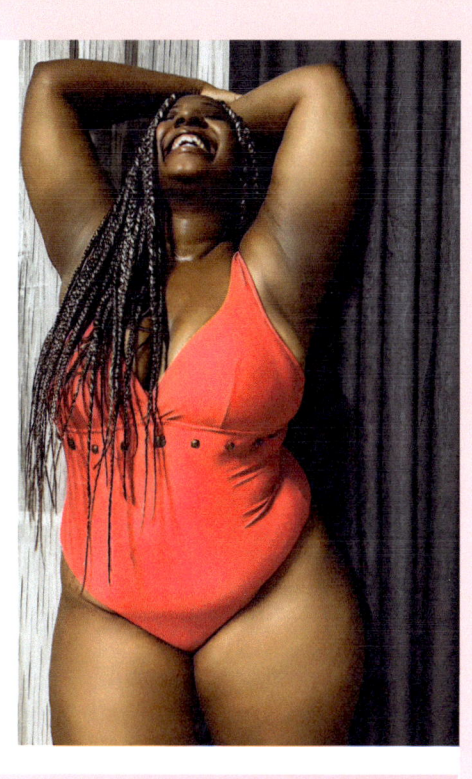
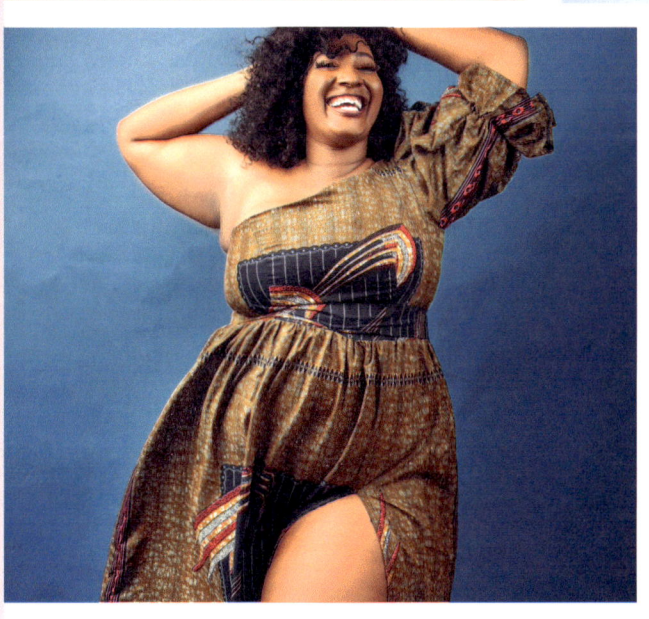
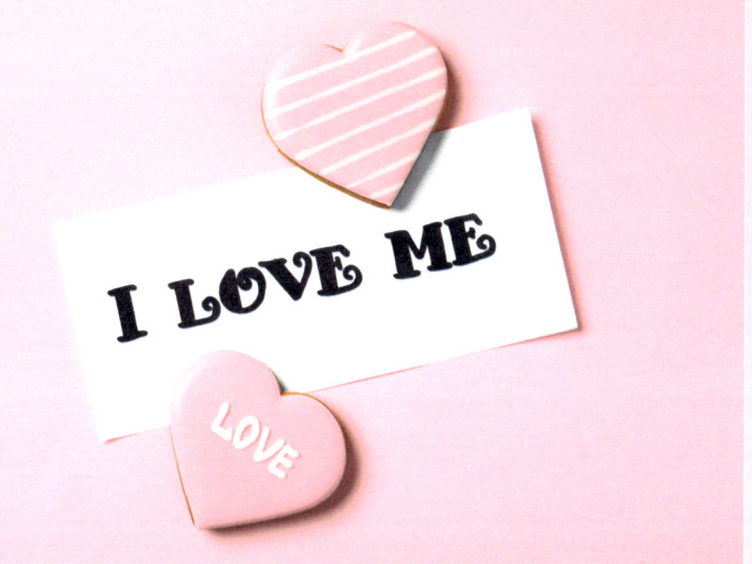

The joy of fitness comes from celebrating progress, not perfection.

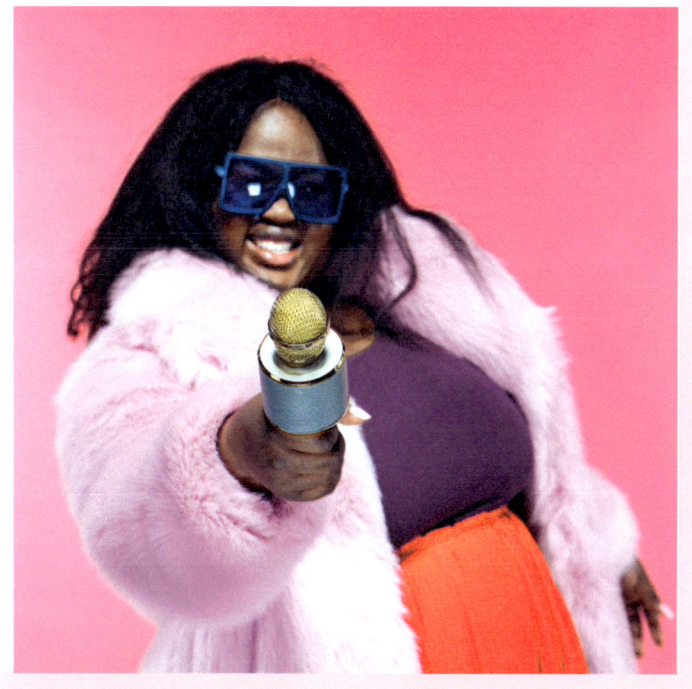

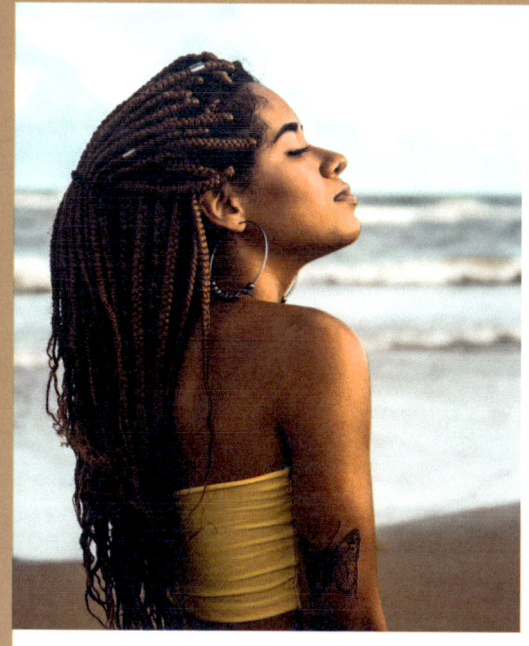
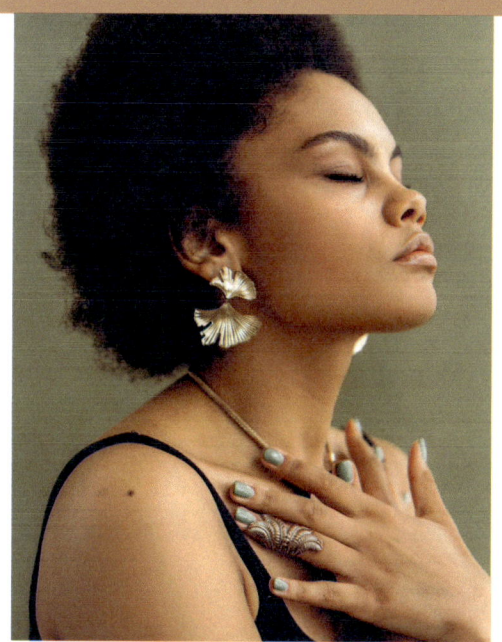
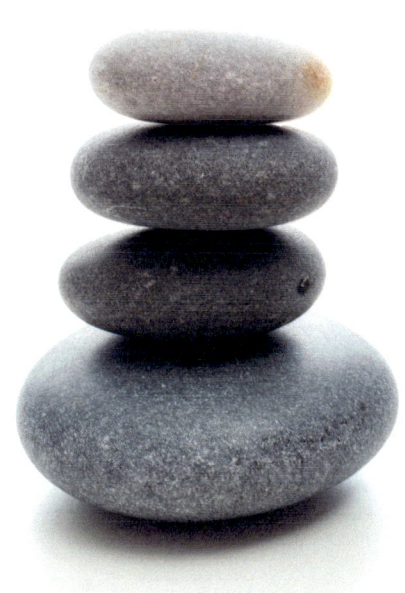

mindfulness

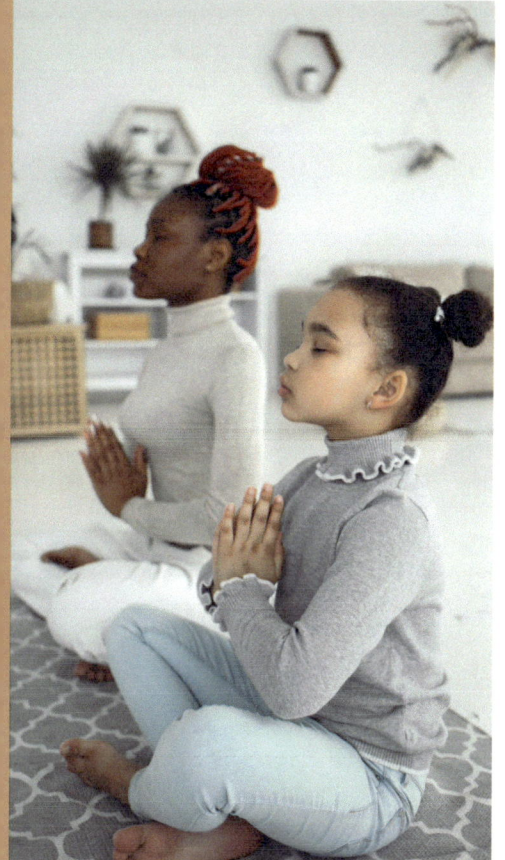
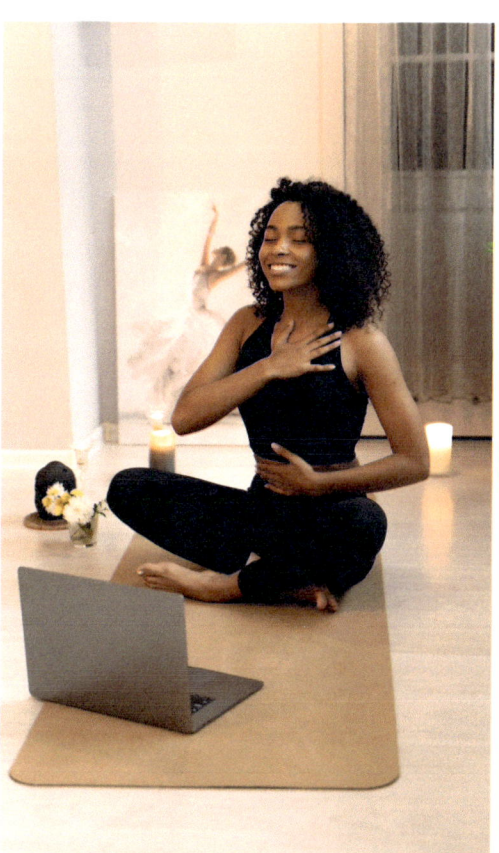
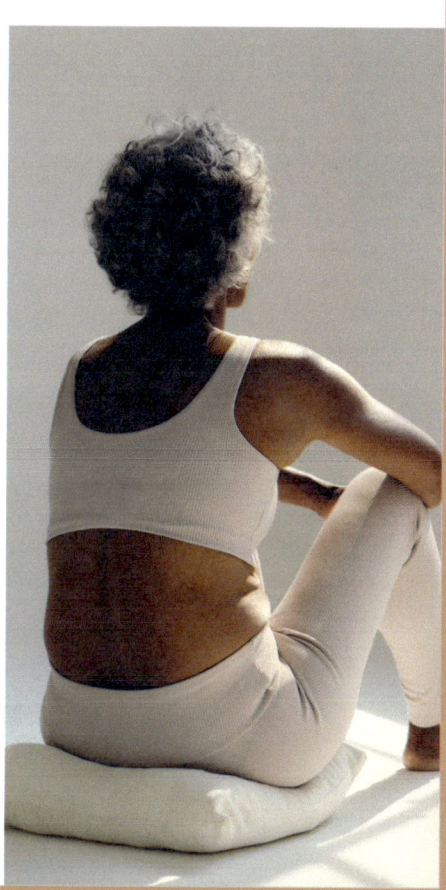

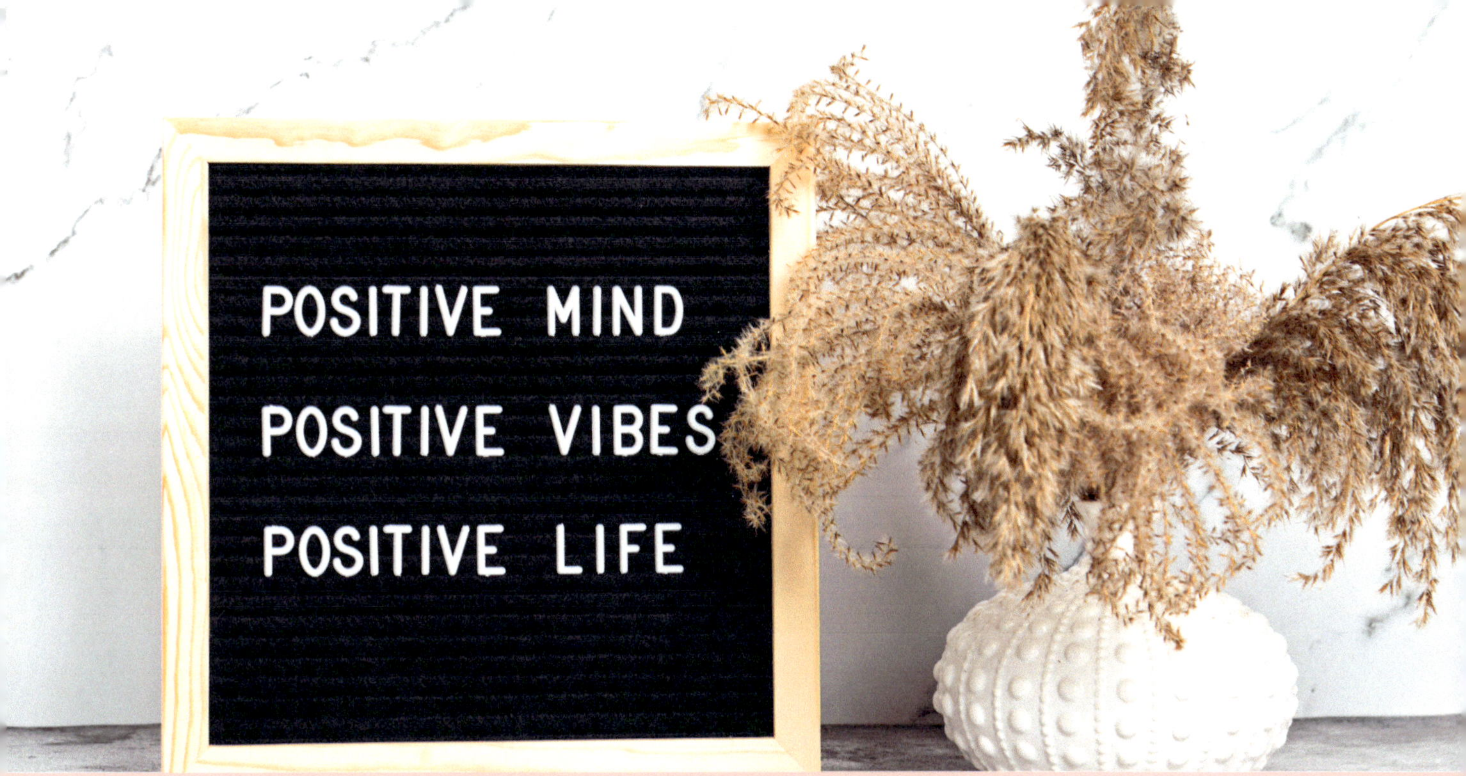

POSITIVE MIND
POSITIVE VIBES
POSITIVE LIFE

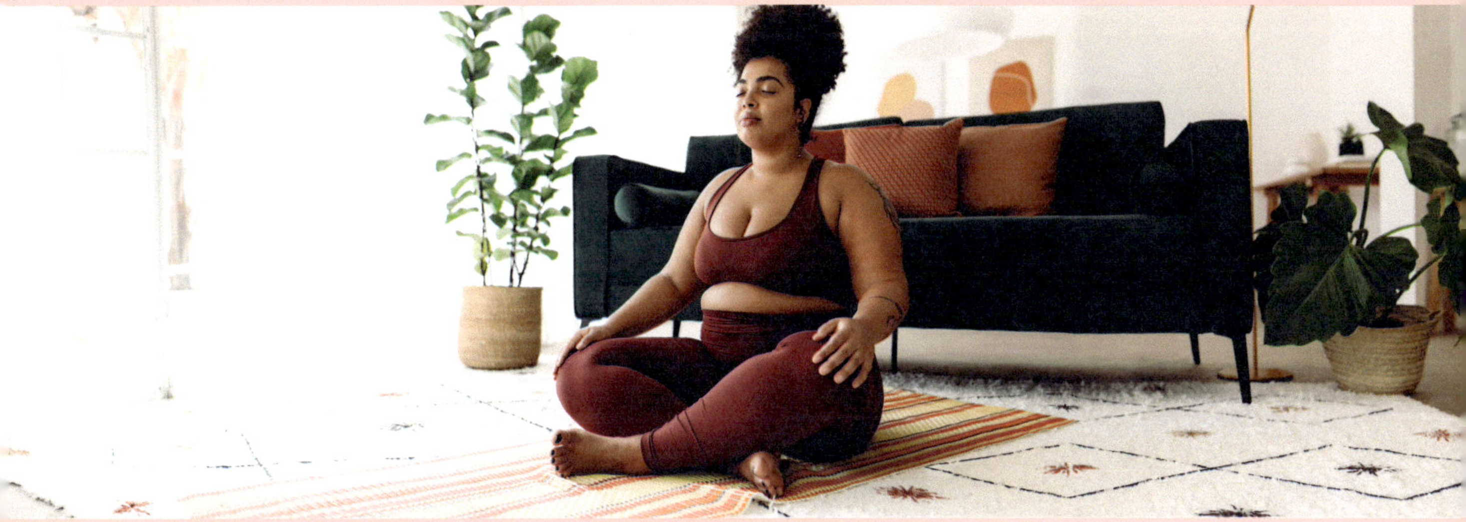

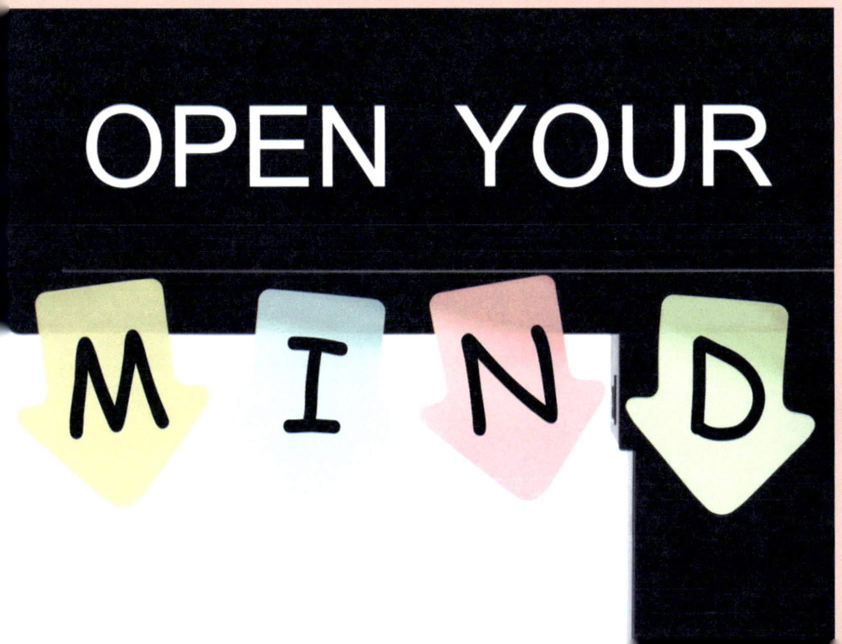

OPEN YOUR MIND

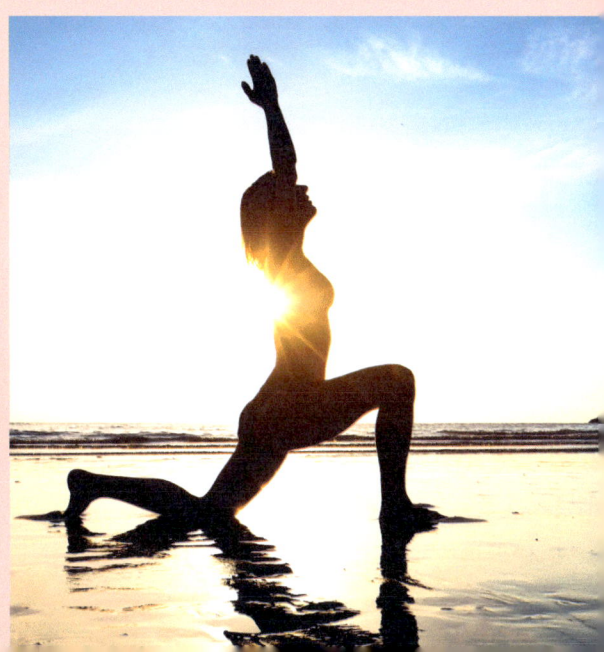

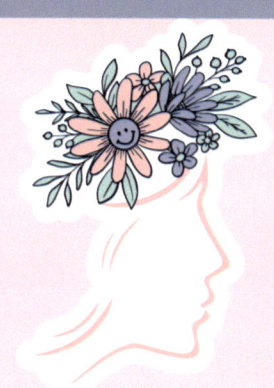
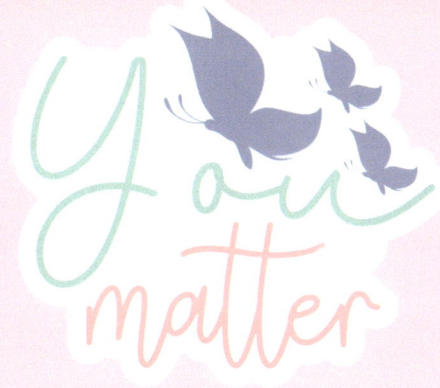
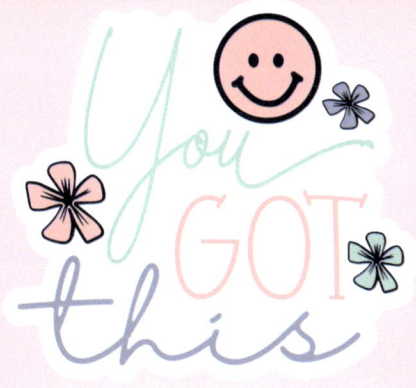
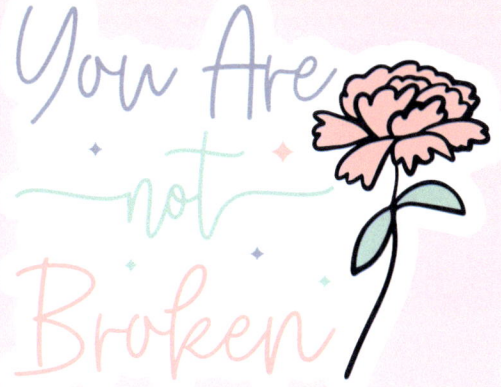
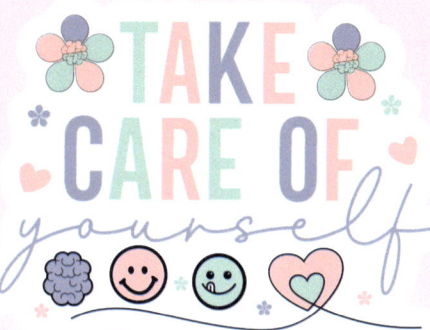
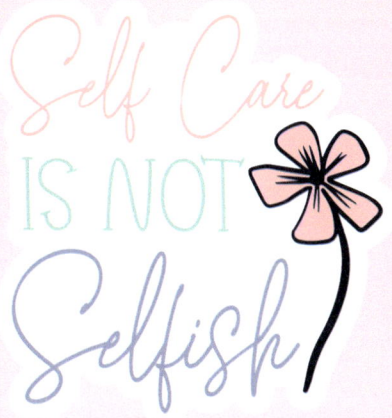
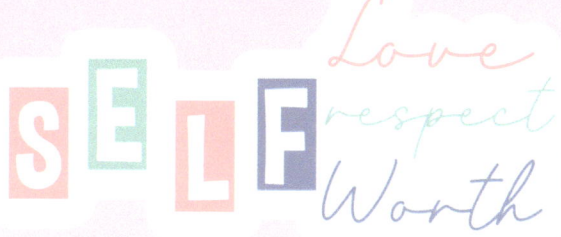
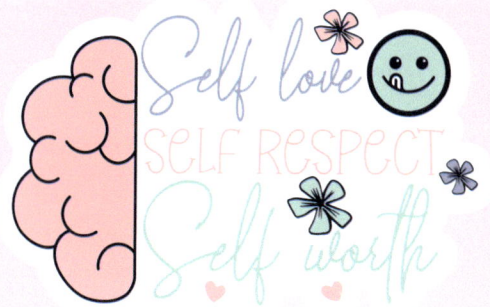
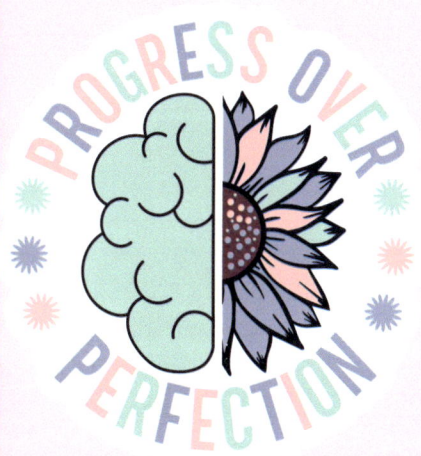
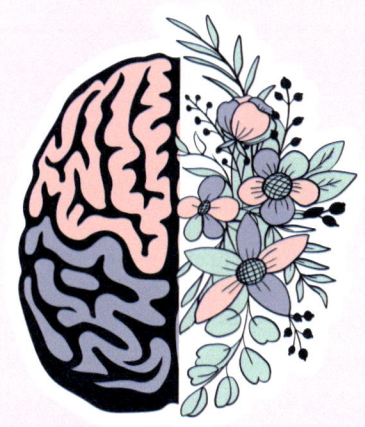
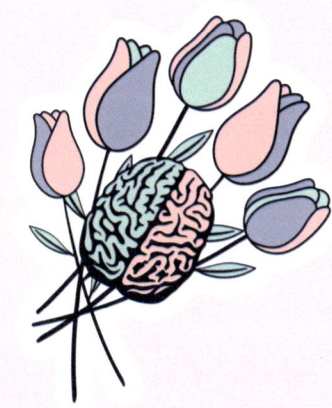
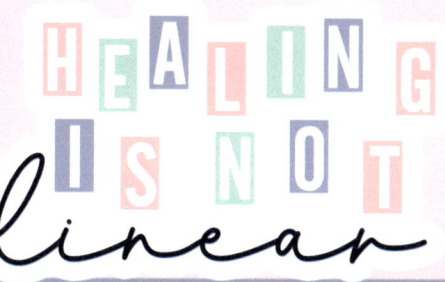
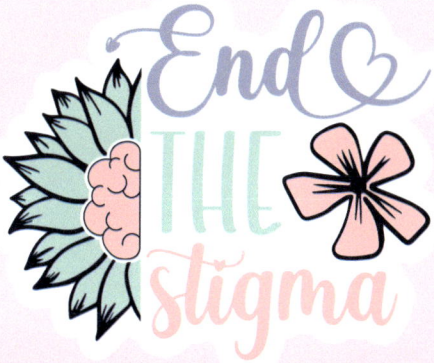
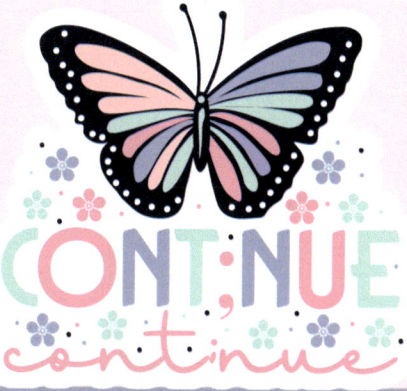

Beauty

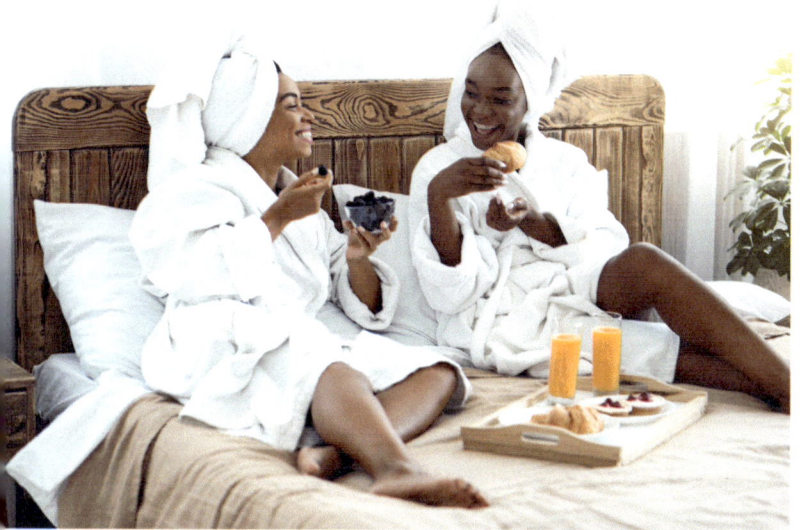
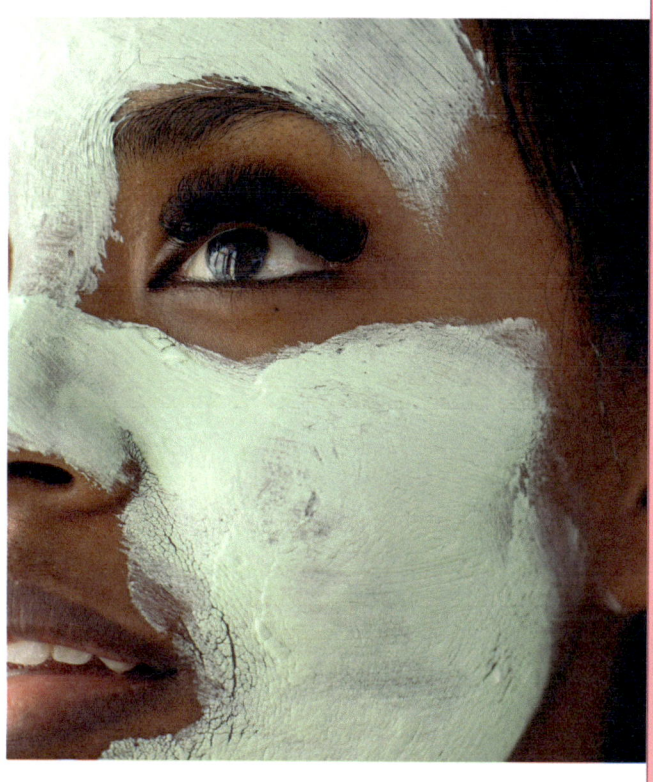
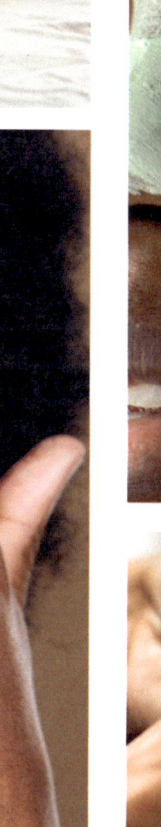
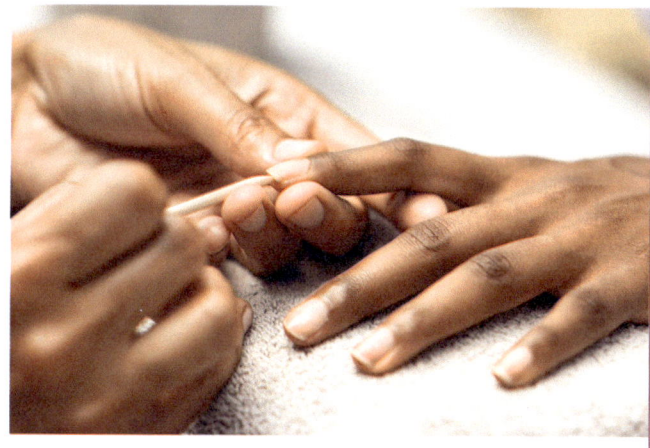
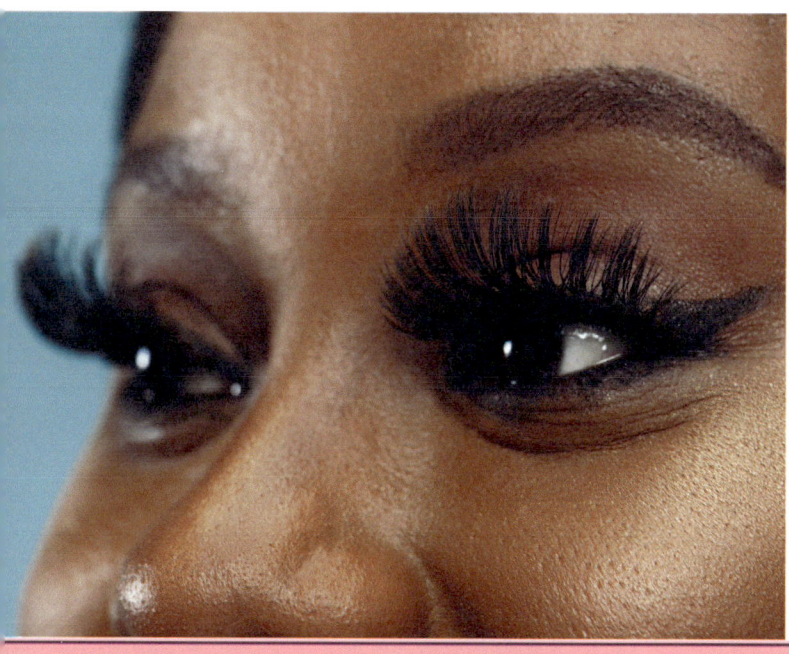

I am Black & Beautiful

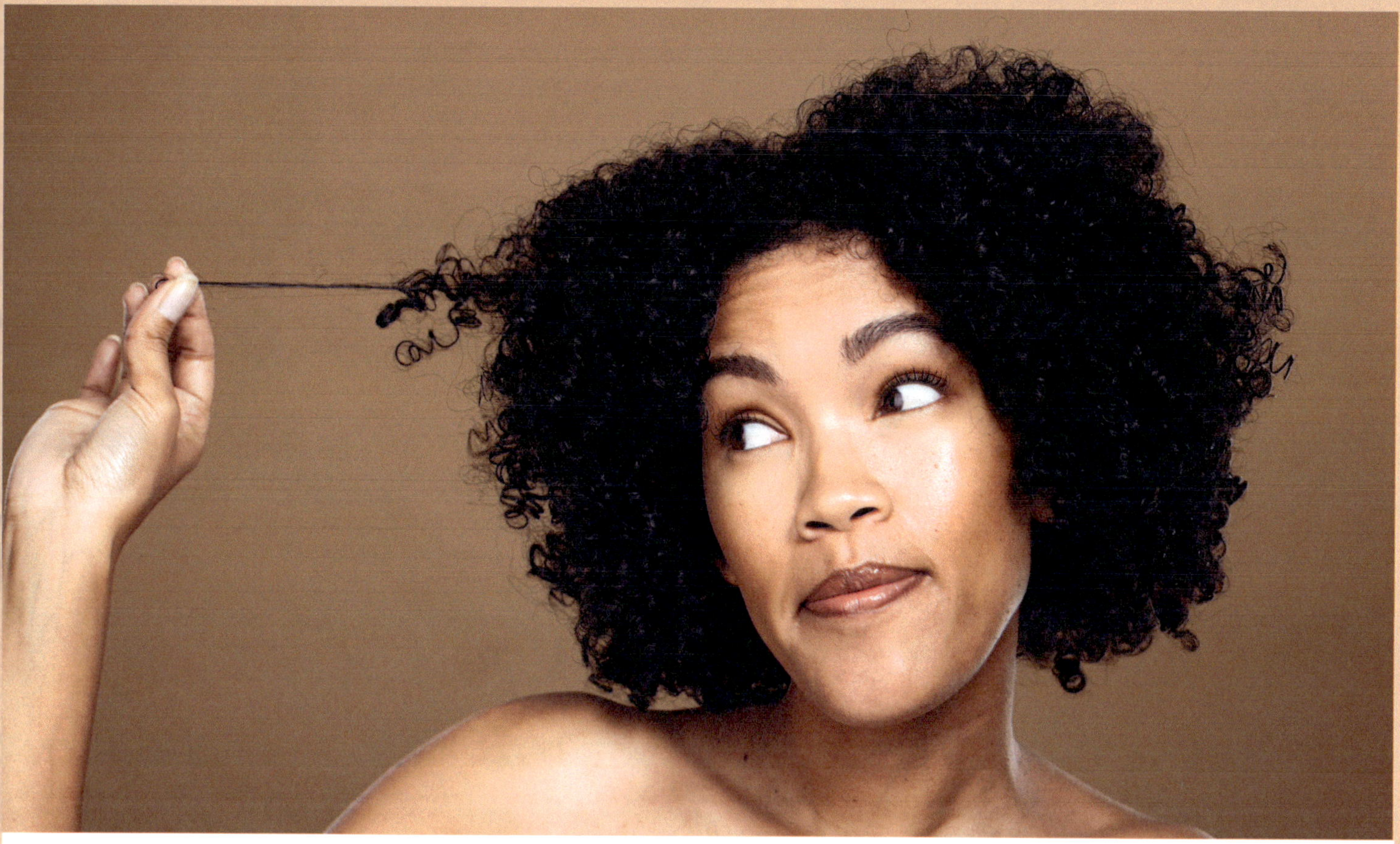

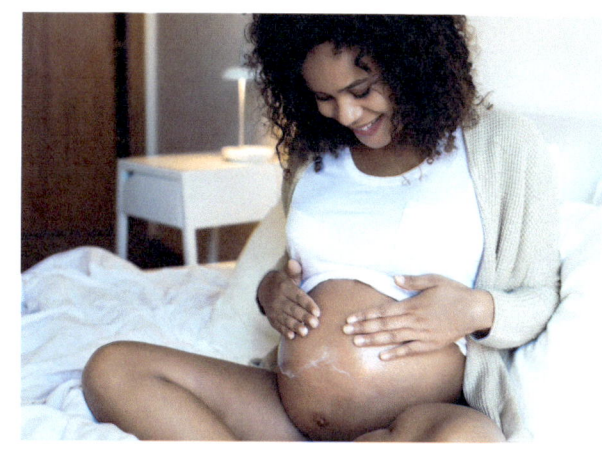

I am confident in my own identity and proud of who I am.

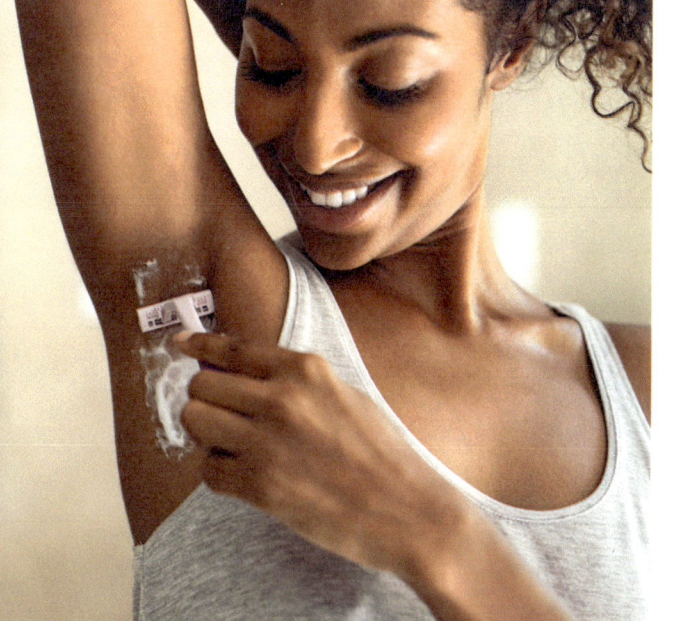

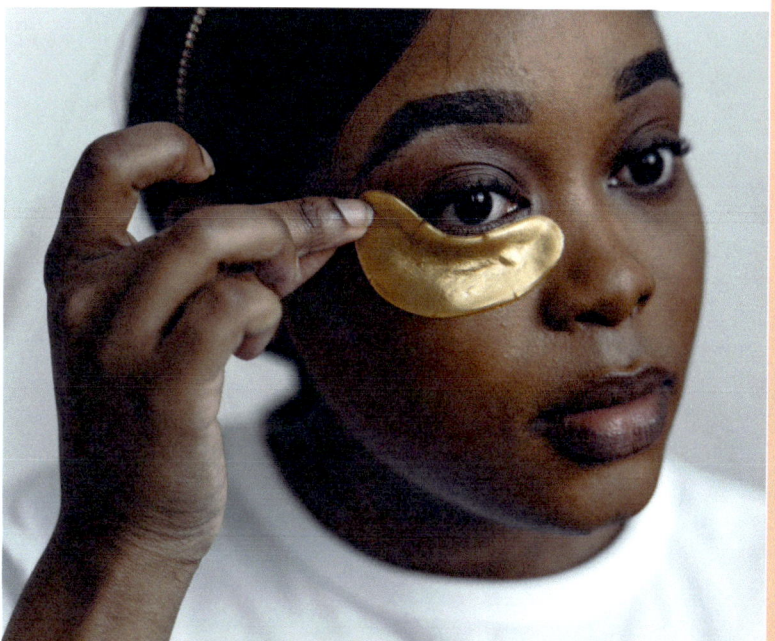

Lifestyle

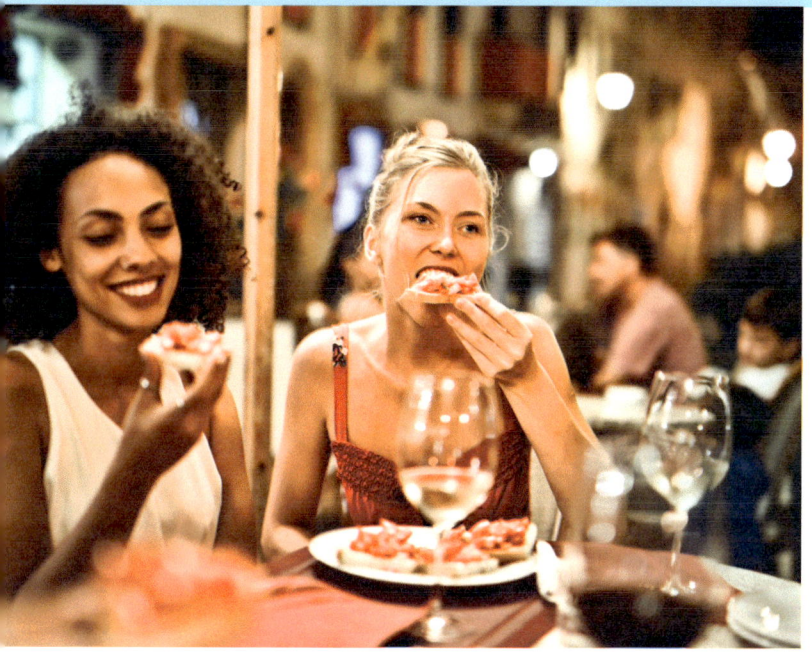

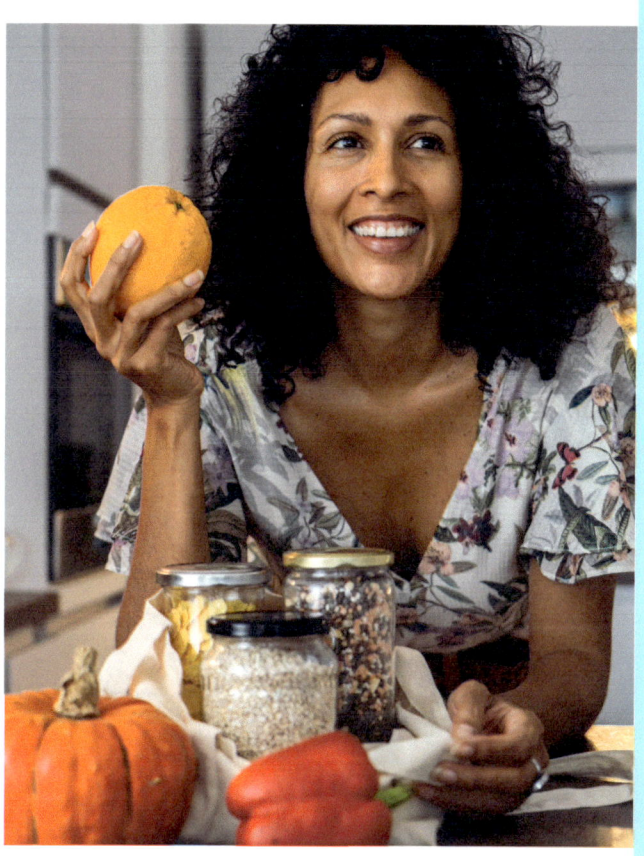

I am capable of creating a life that aligns with my values and brings me joy and fulfillment.

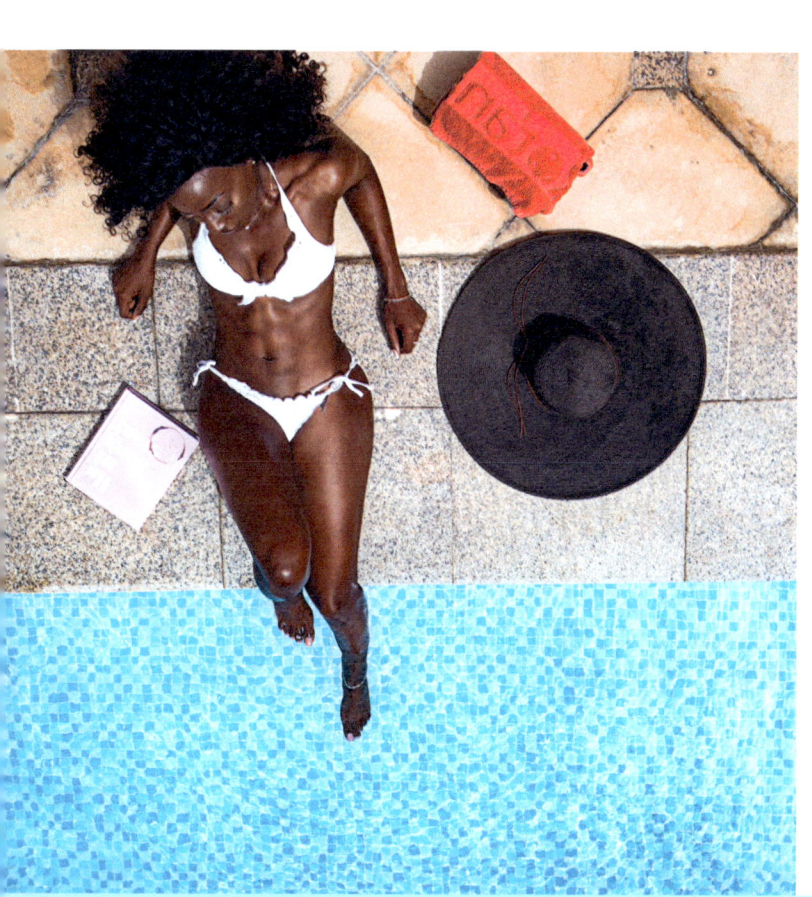

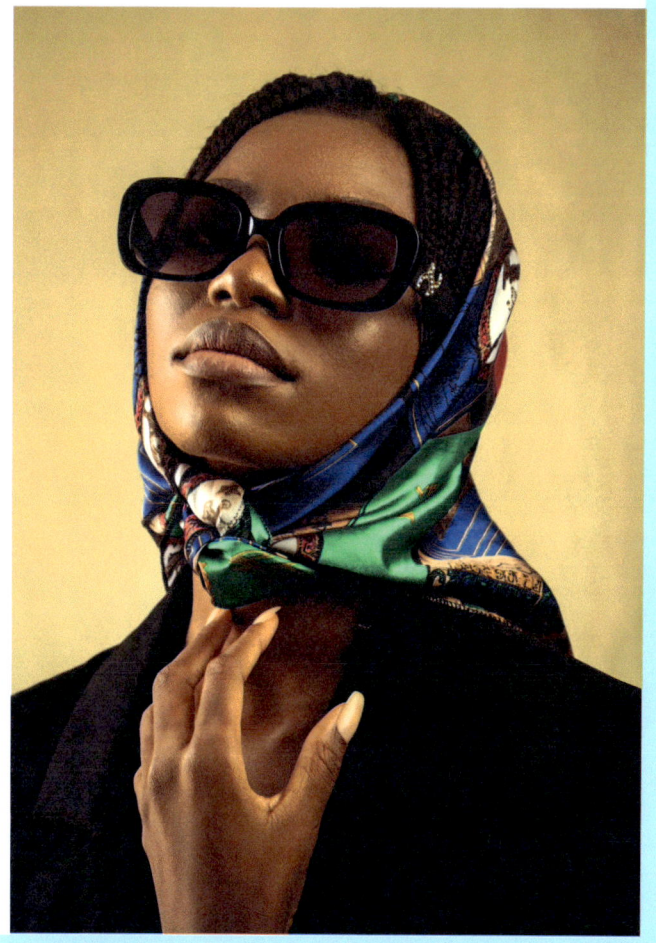

I am worthy of being surrounded by people who uplift and inspire me.

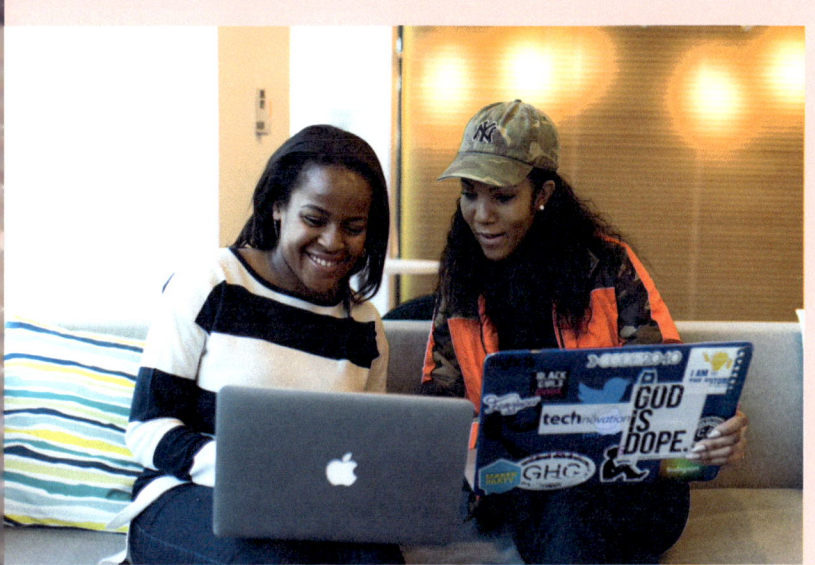
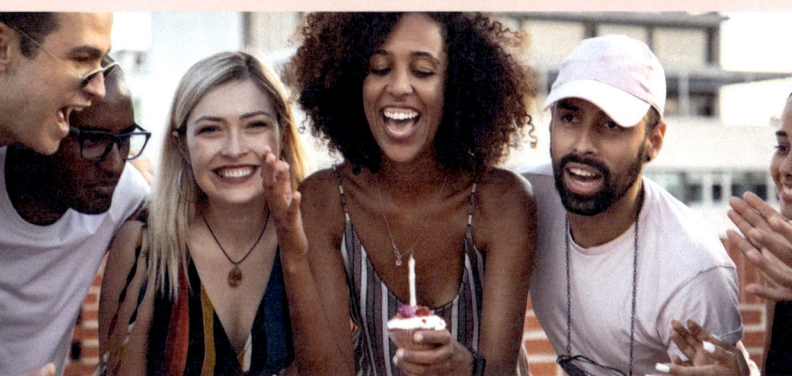
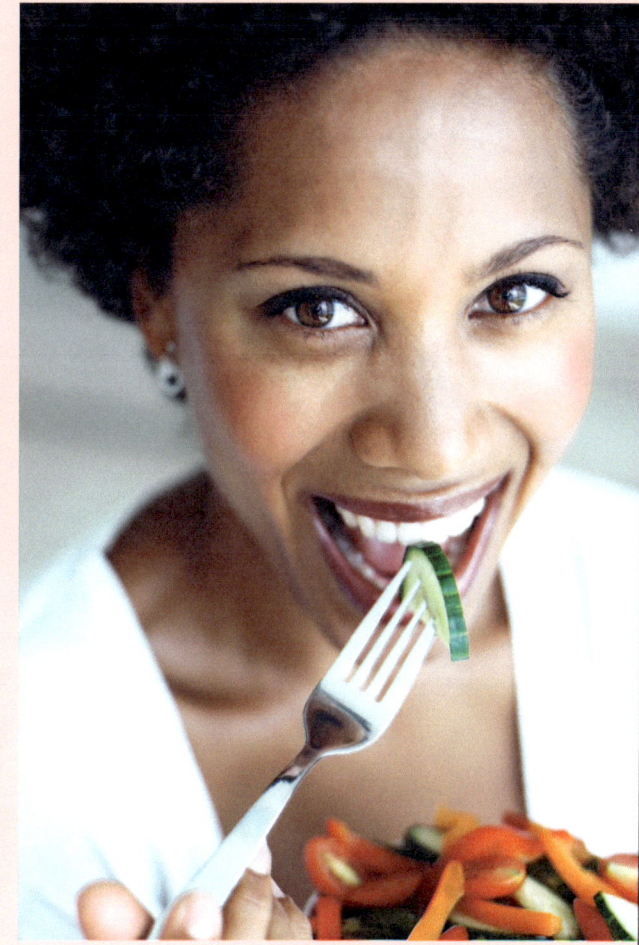
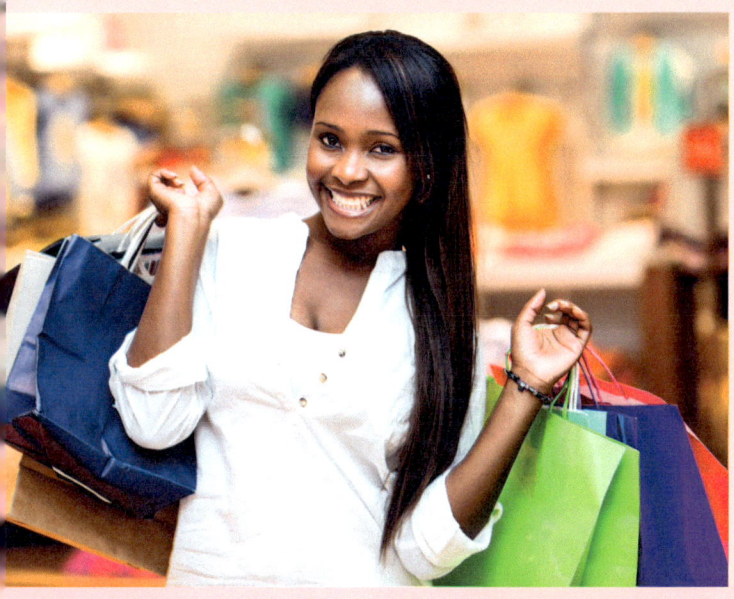
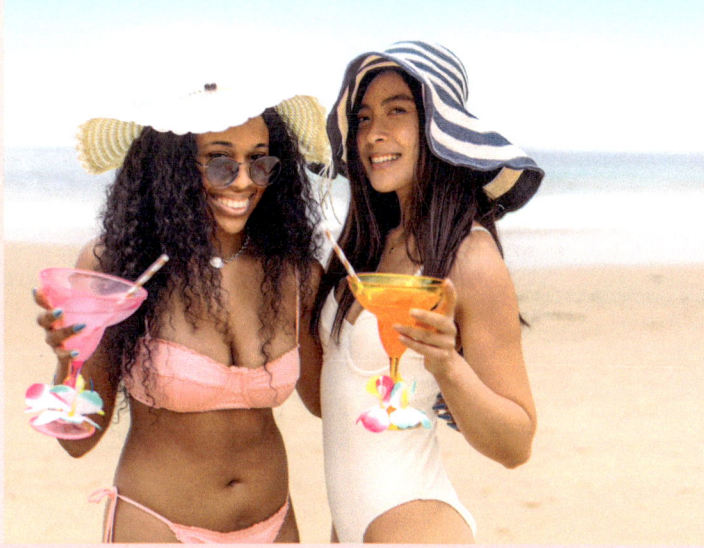

I am strong, Nothing is Impossible

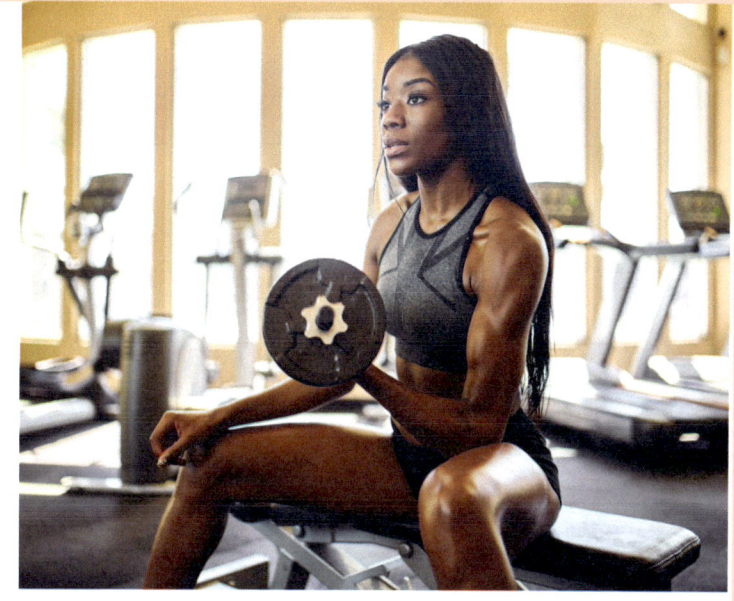
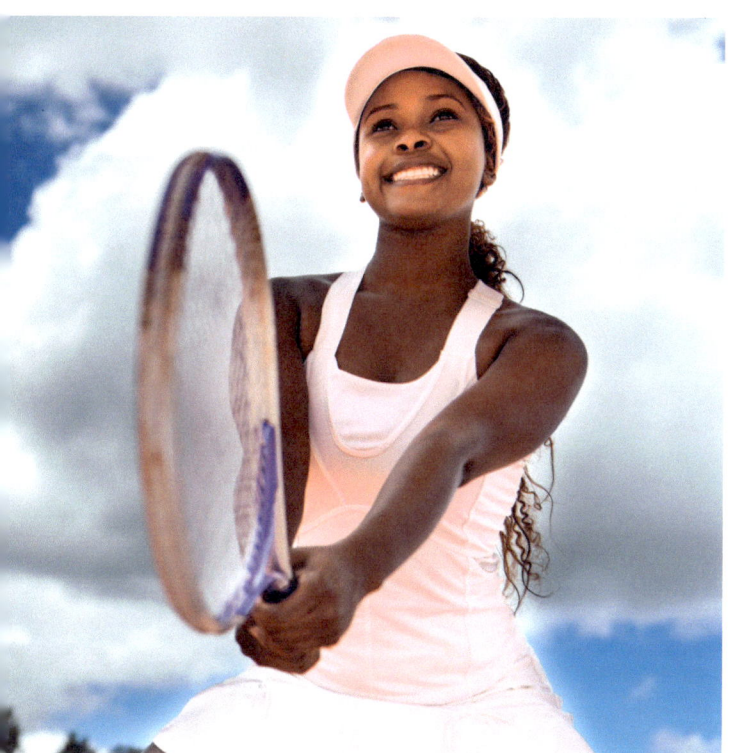
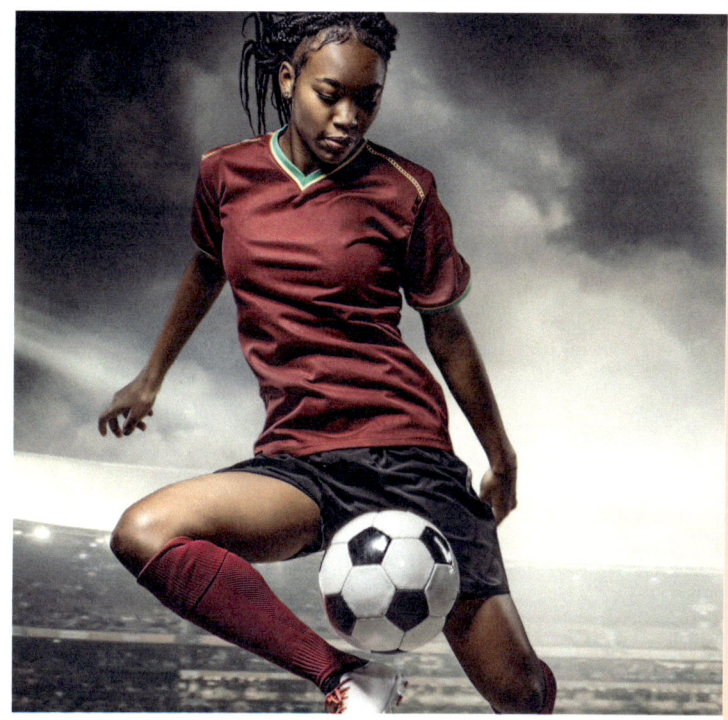
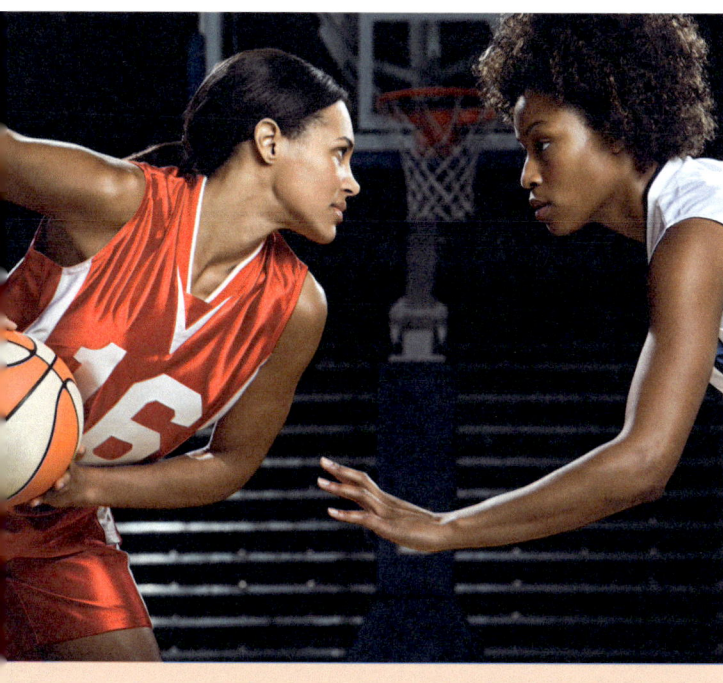
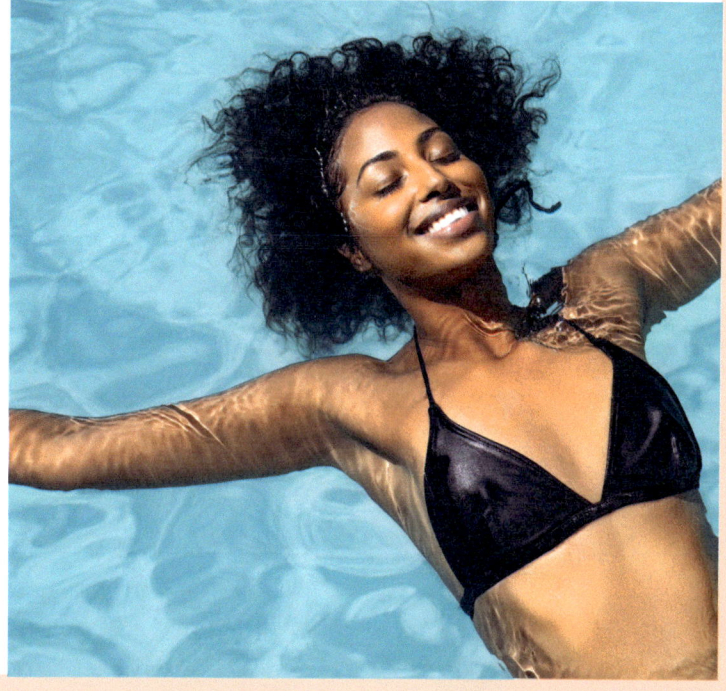

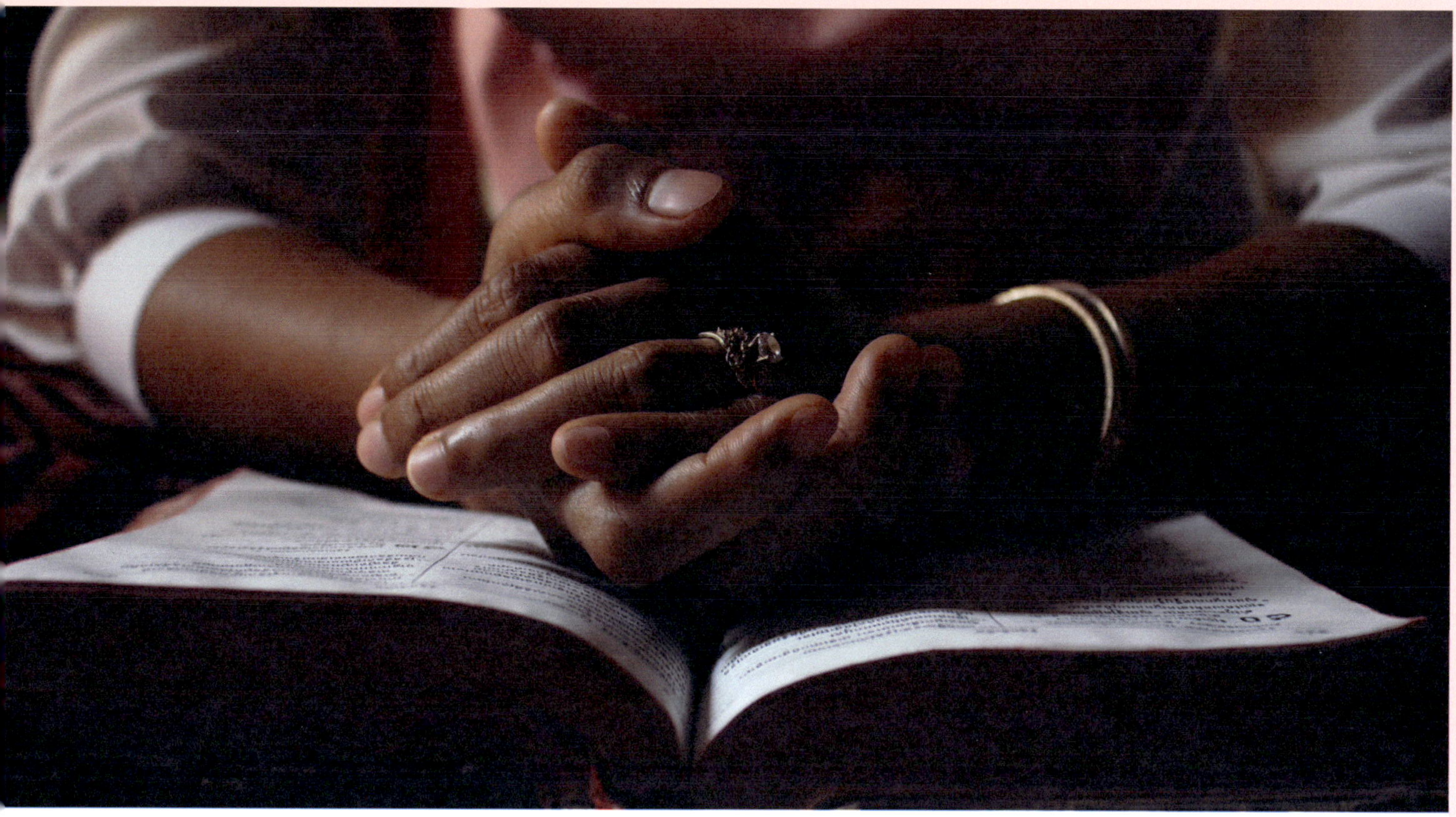

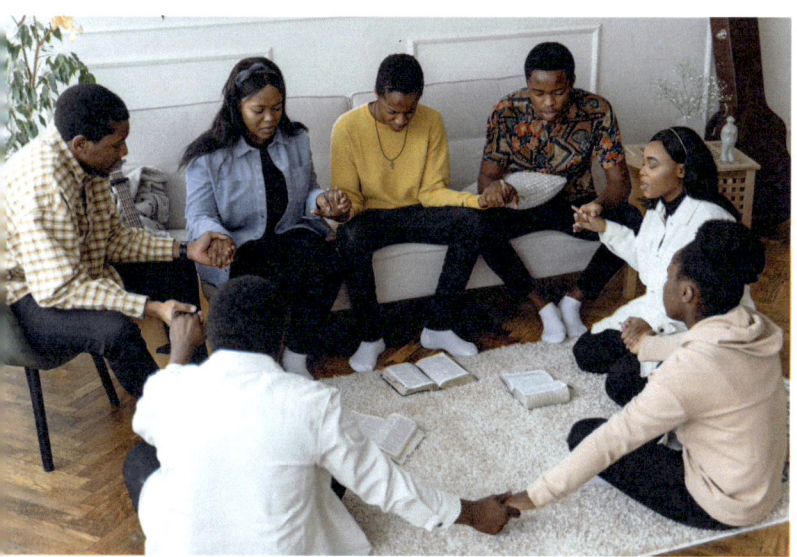

Prayer Gives Comfort & Hope.

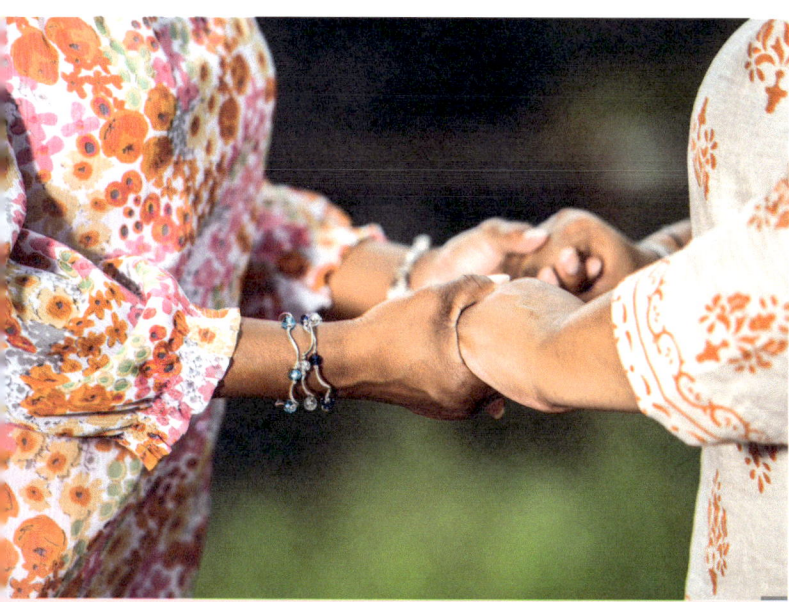
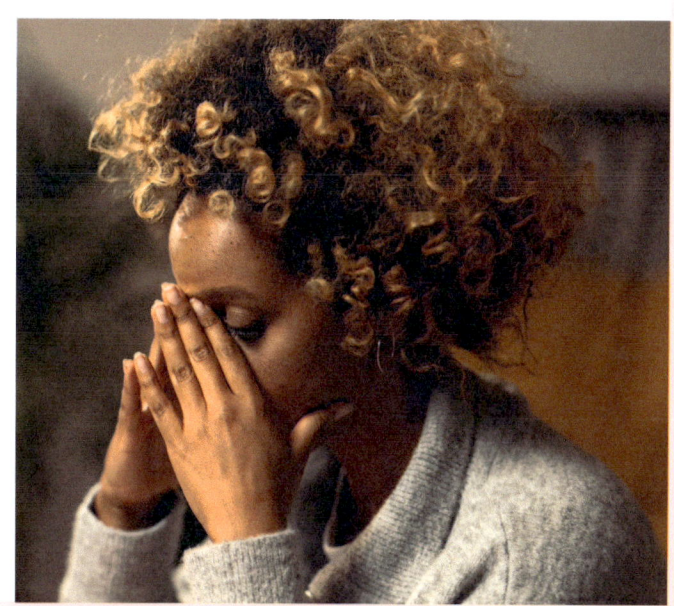

Prayer brings peace, Strength, and divine guidance.

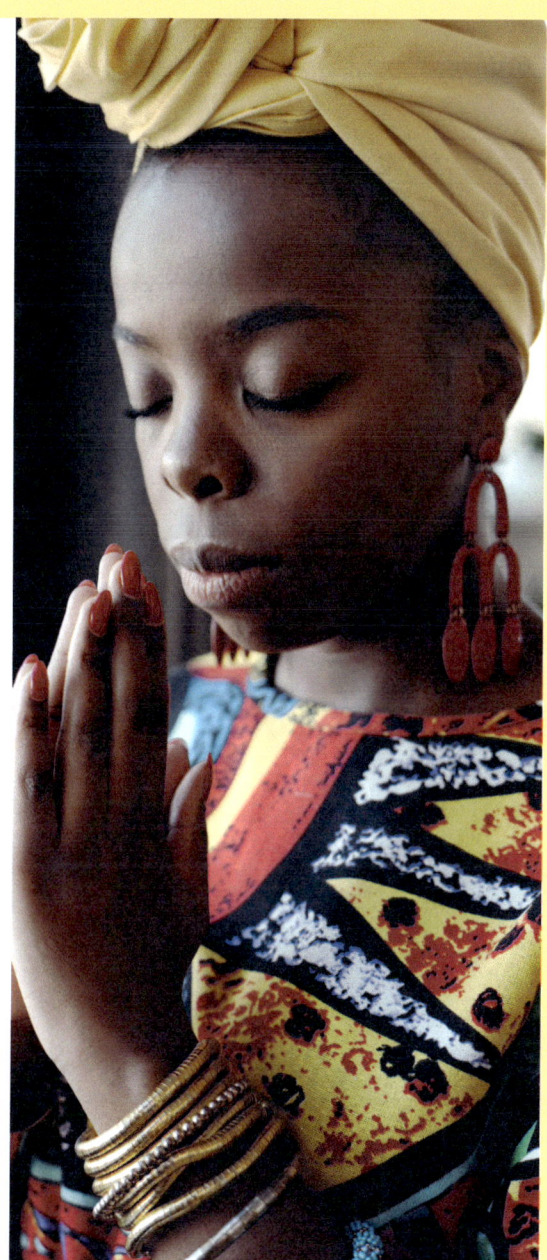
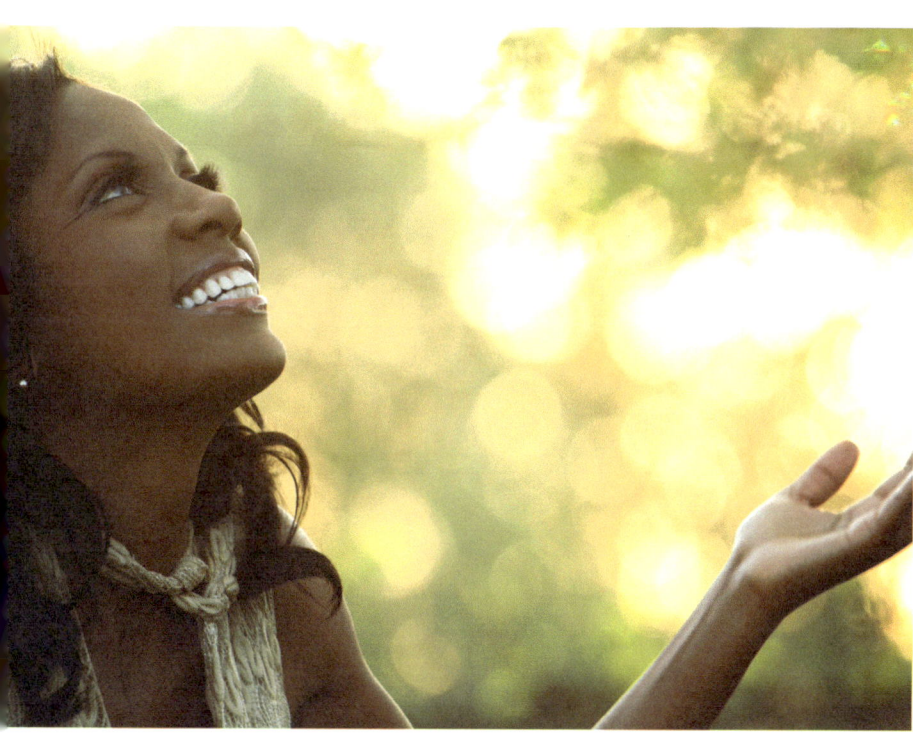

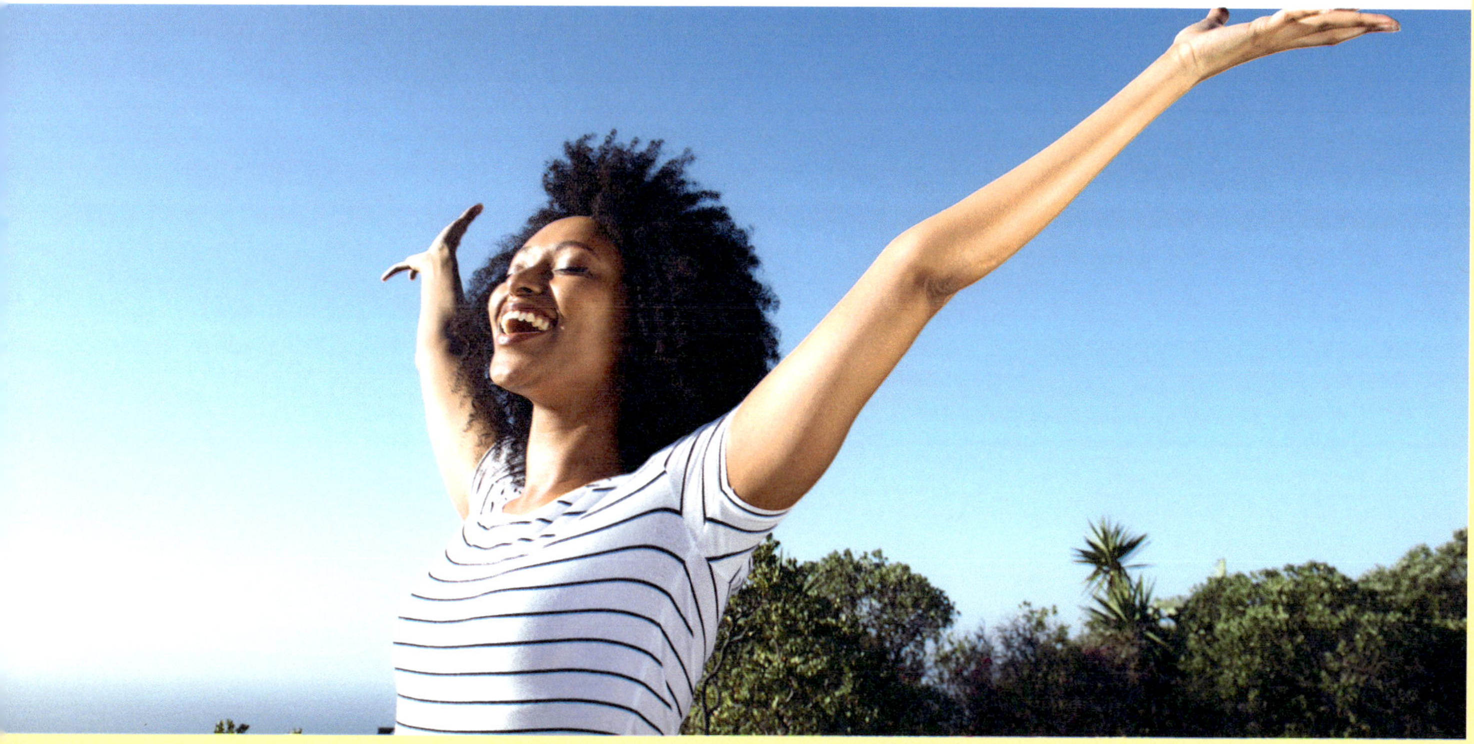

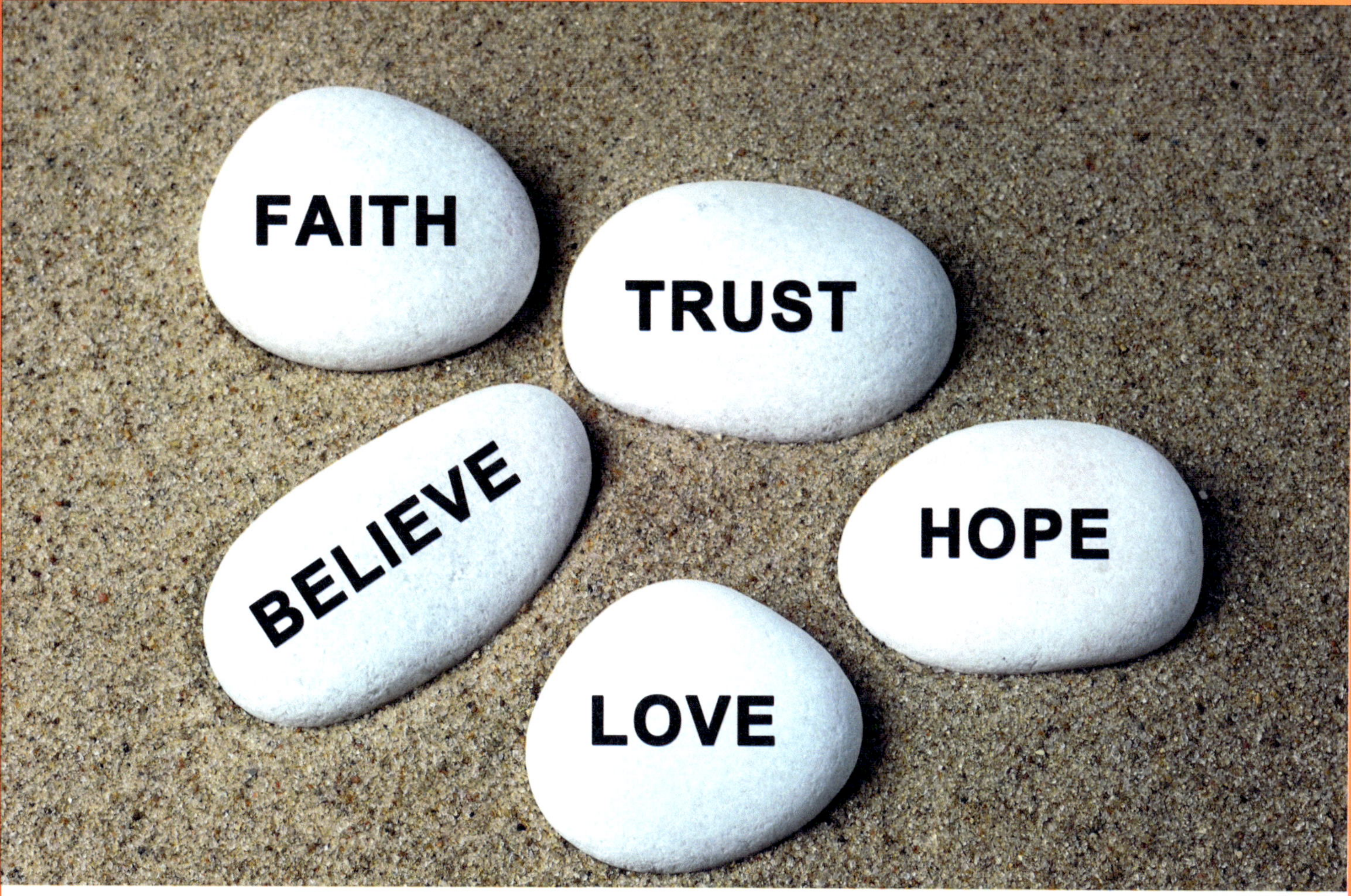

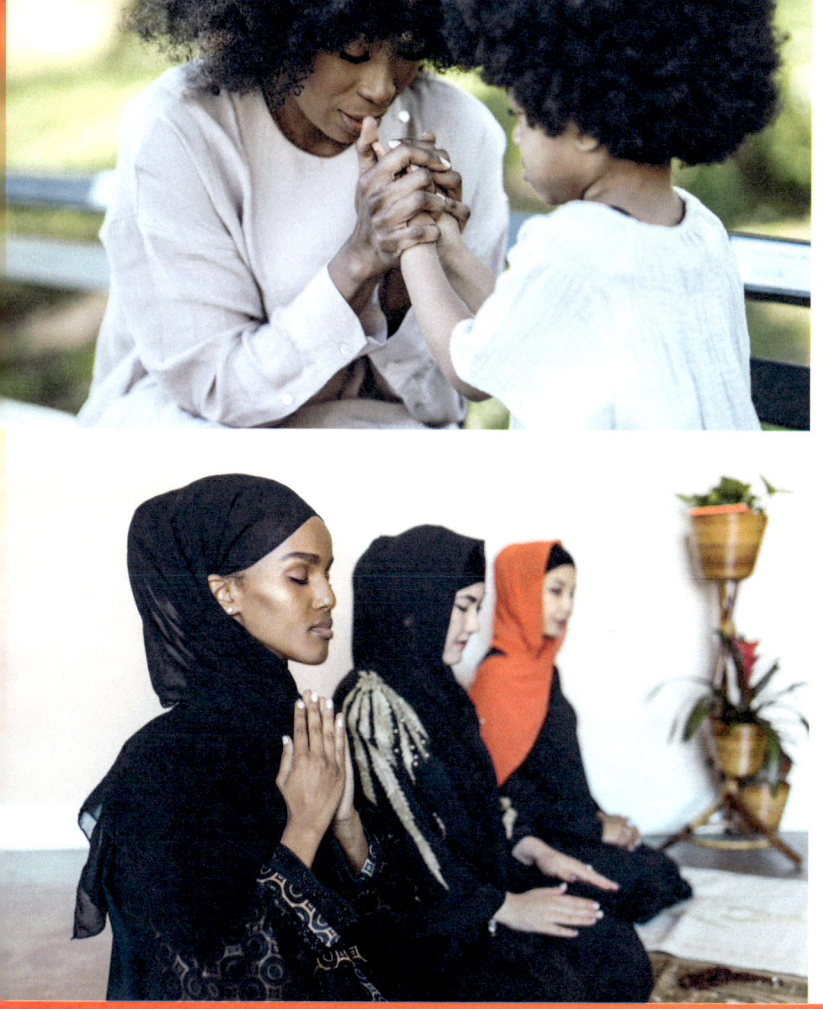
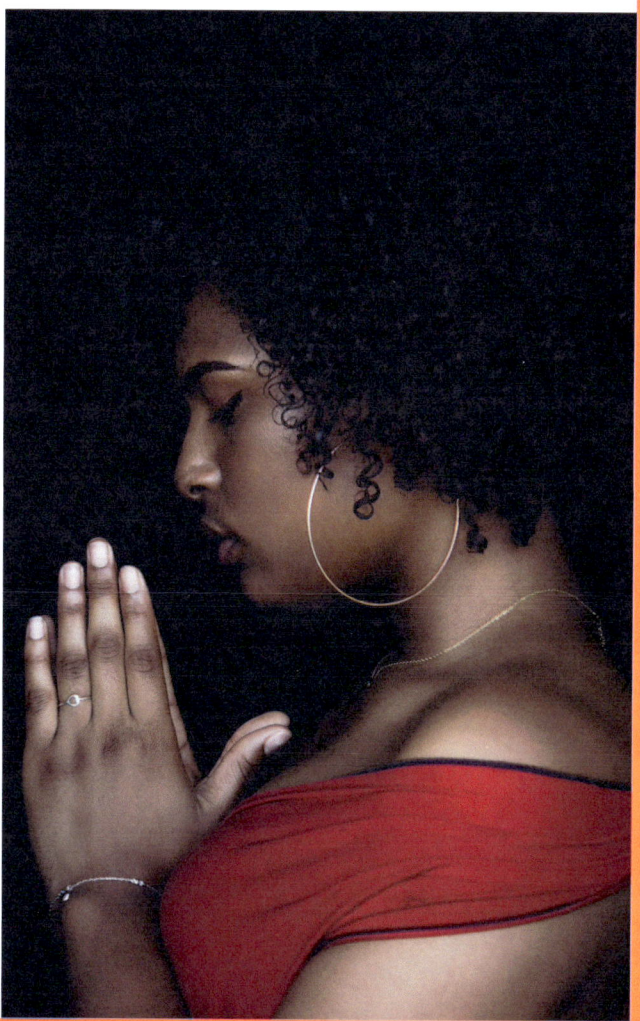

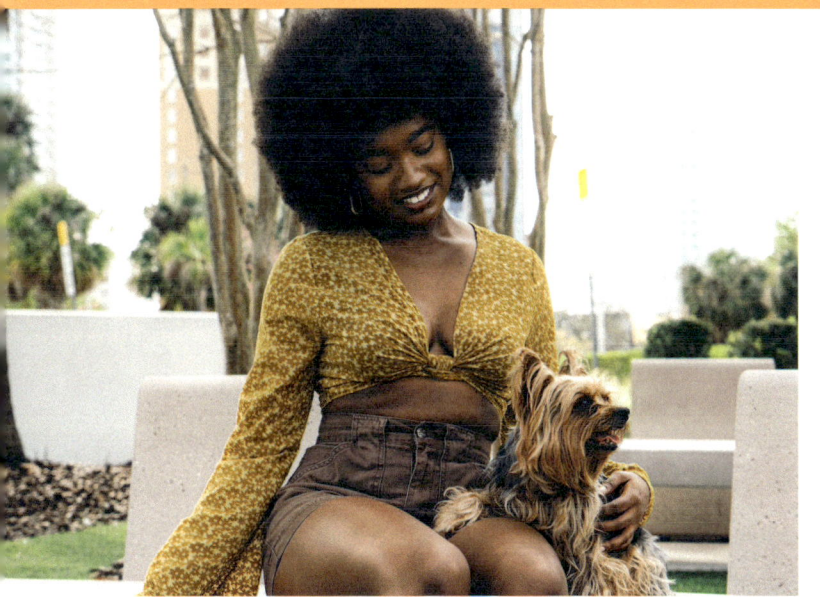

Love, Trust, Joy.

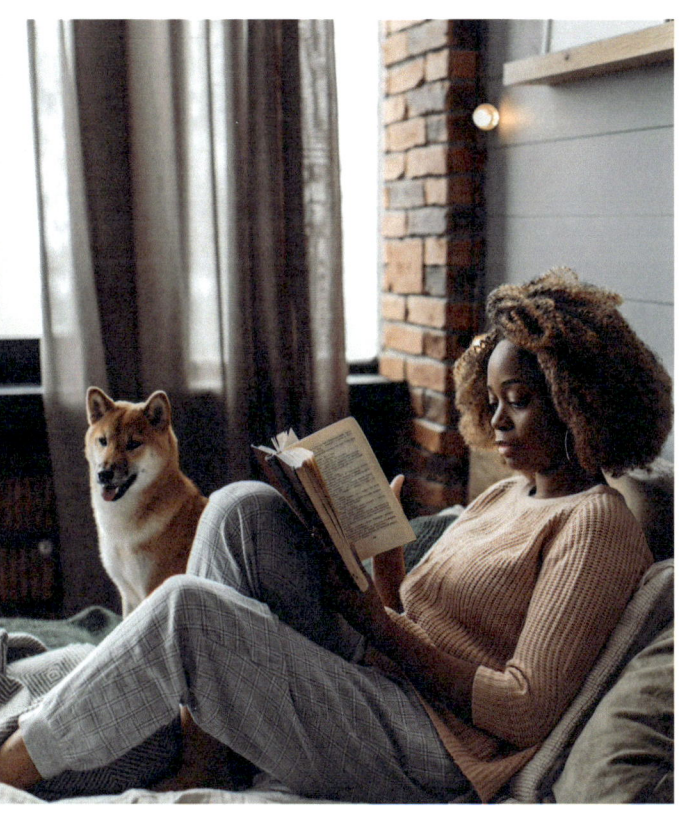
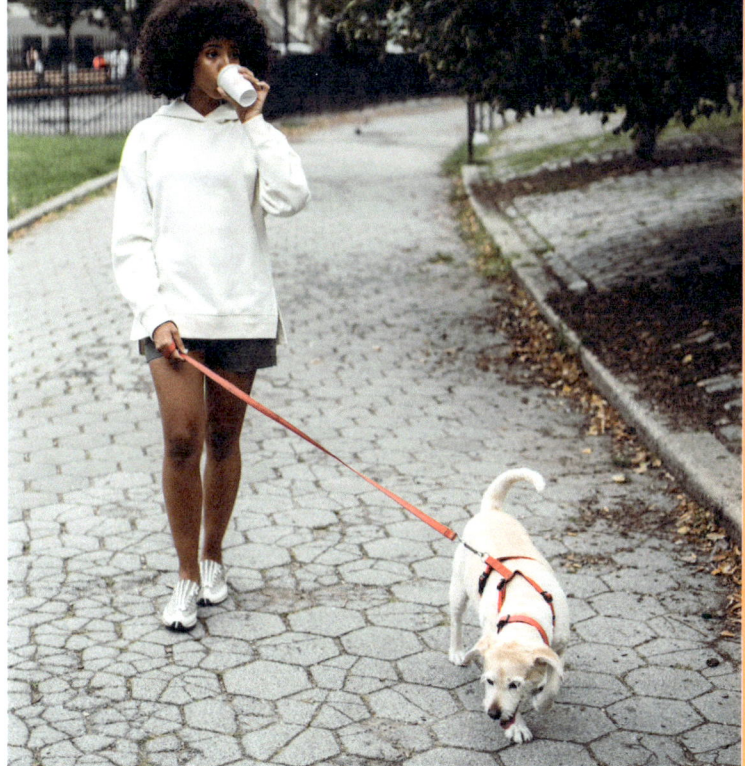
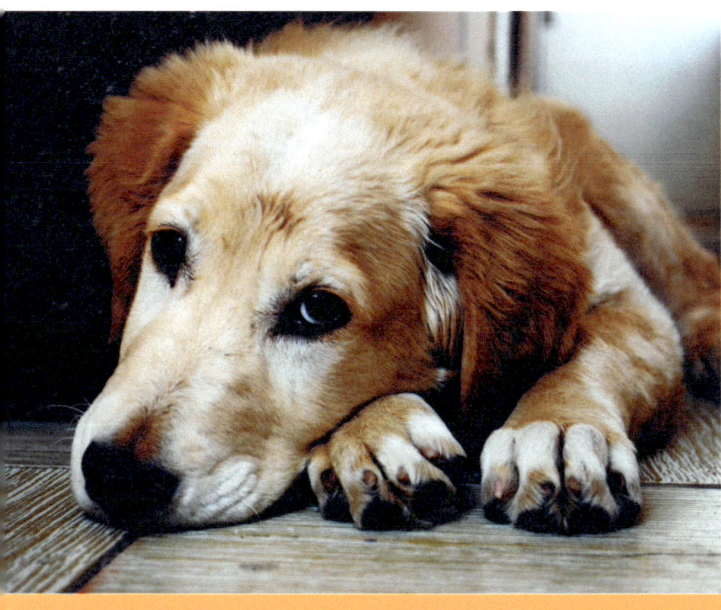
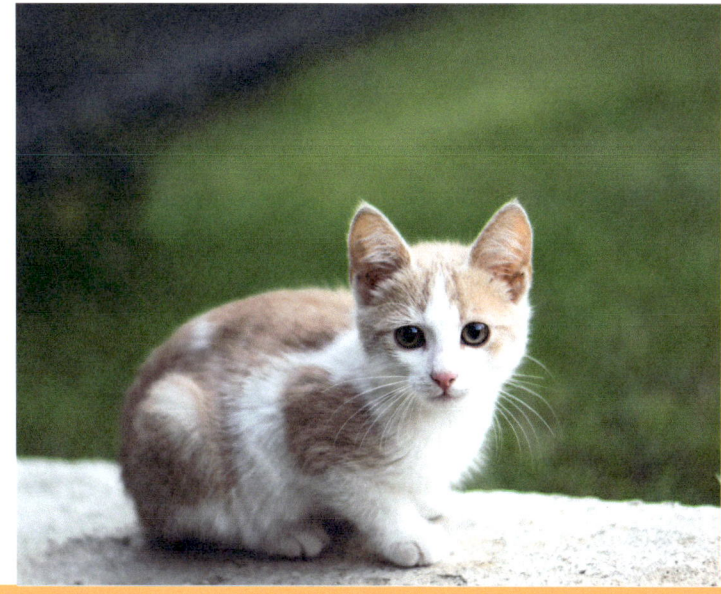

Joy, Loyalty & Unconditional love

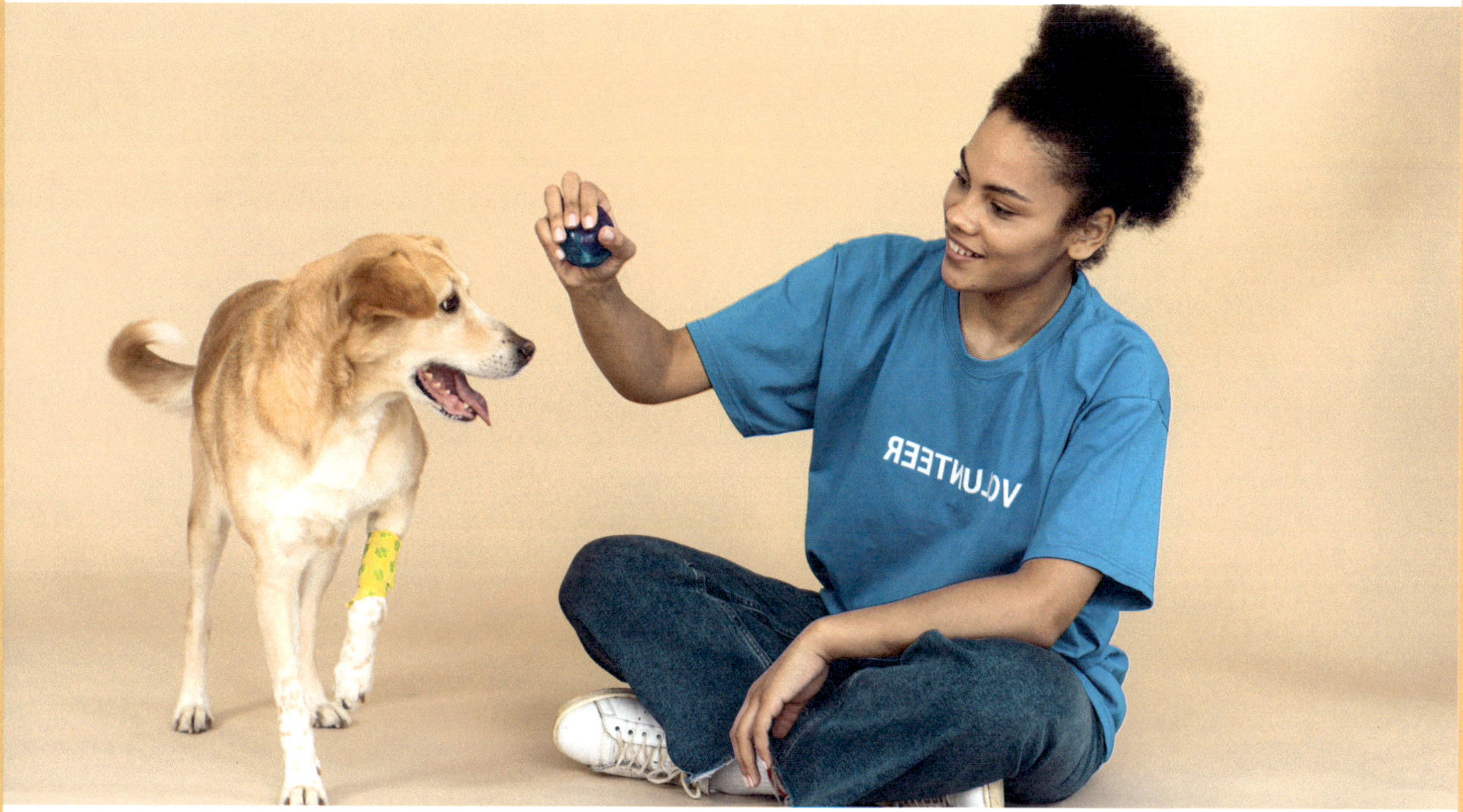

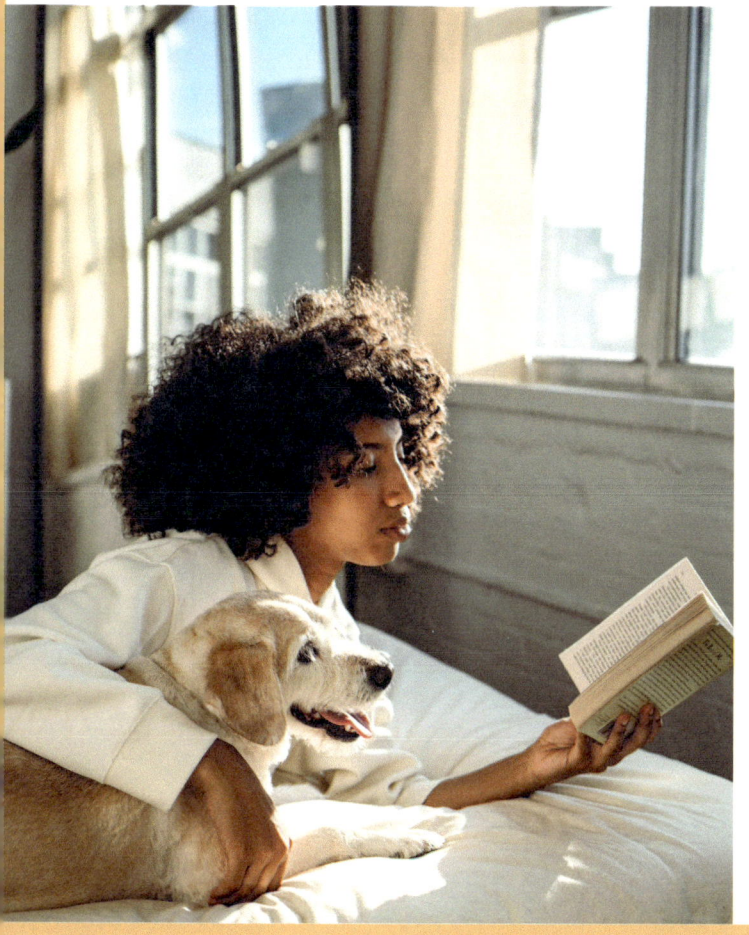
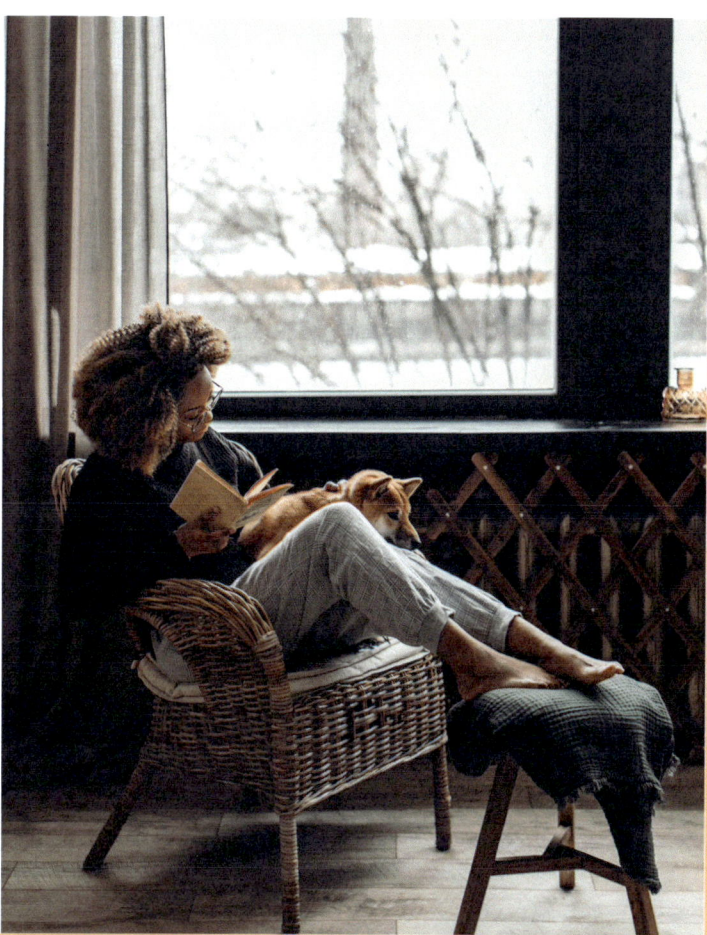

Dream Vacations

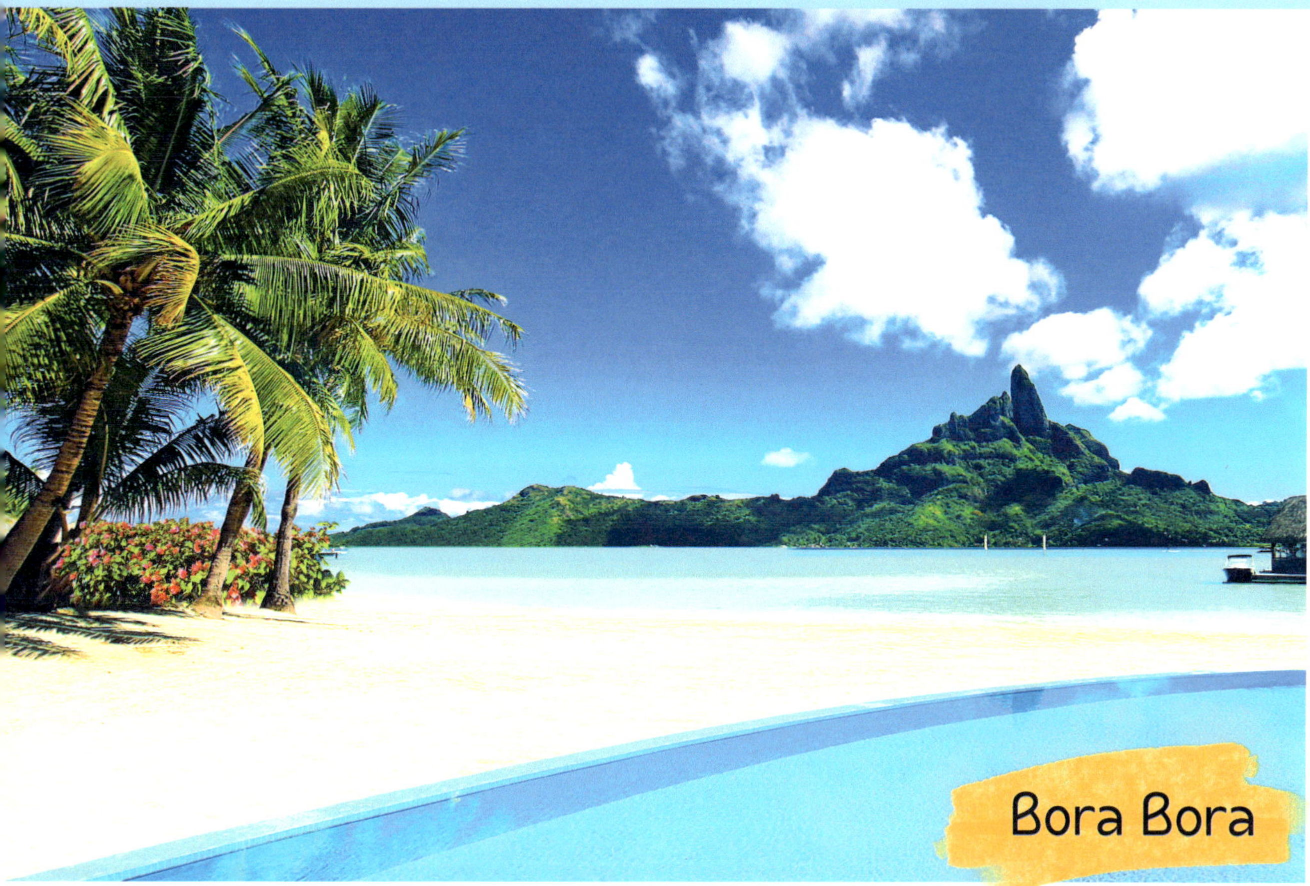

Bora Bora

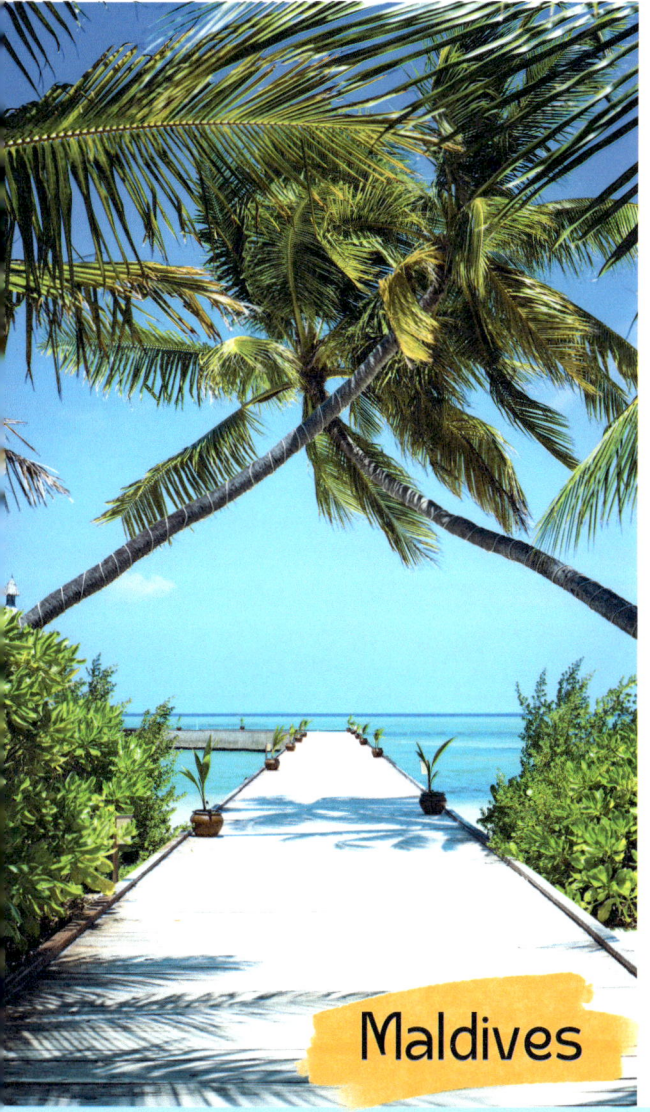

Maldives

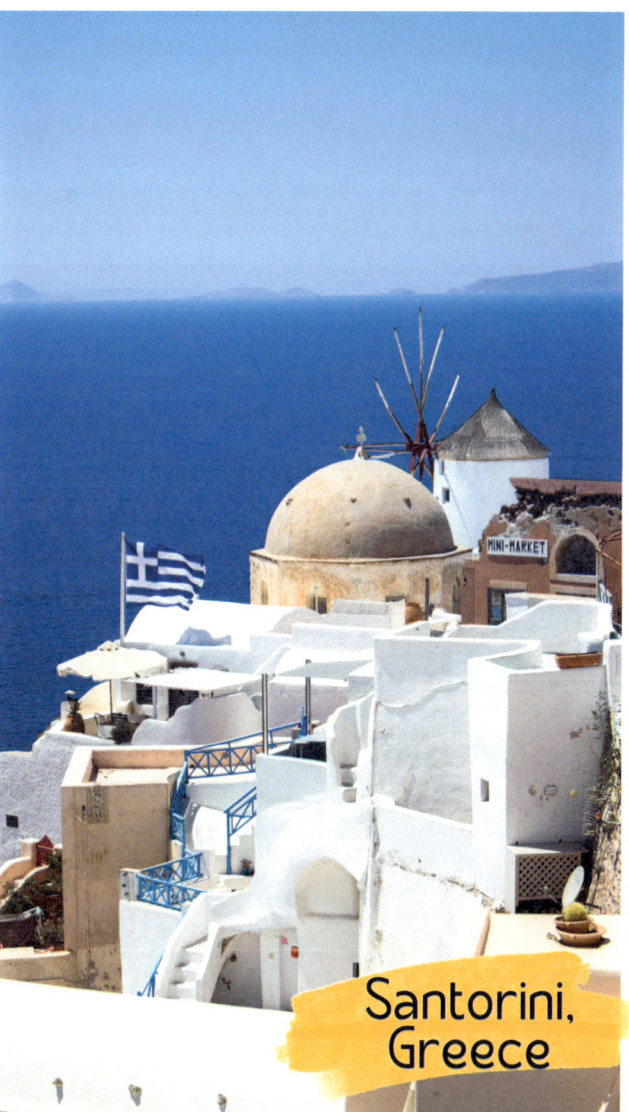

Santorini, Greece

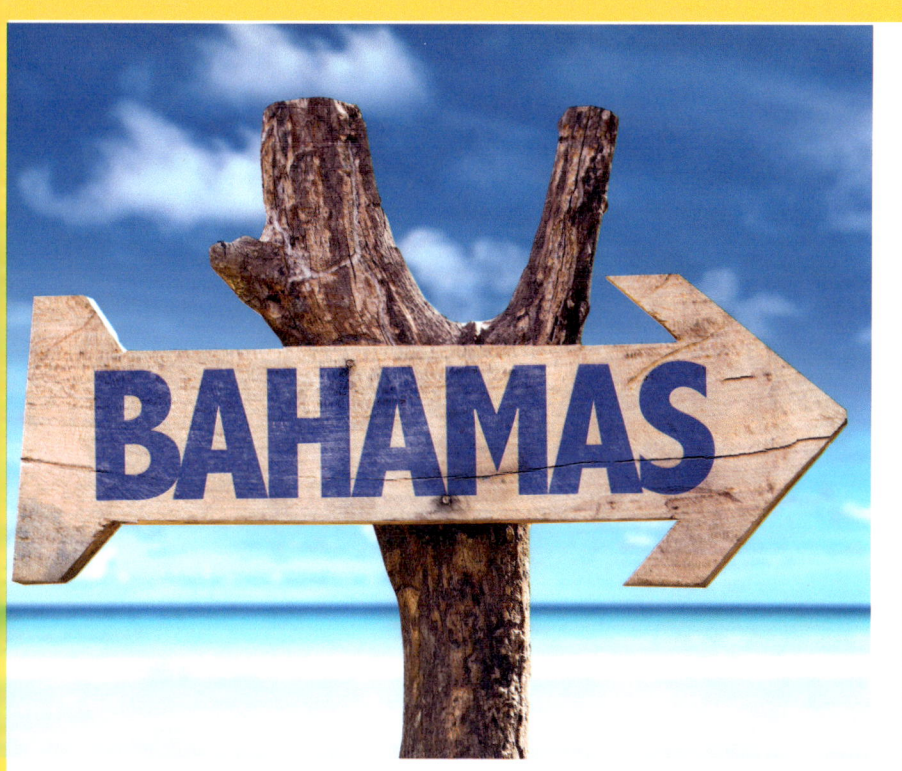
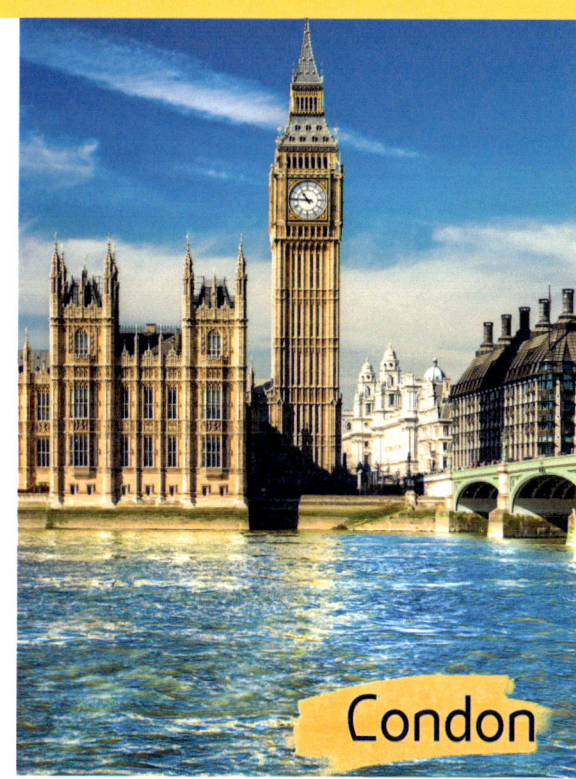

Condon

Italy

Paris

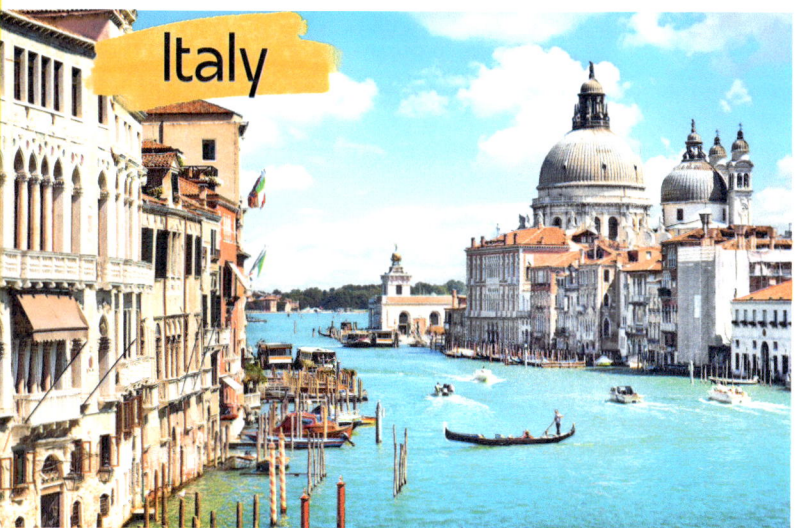
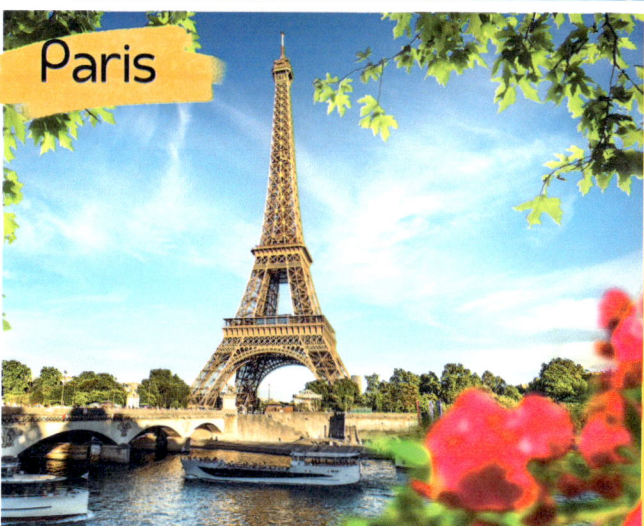
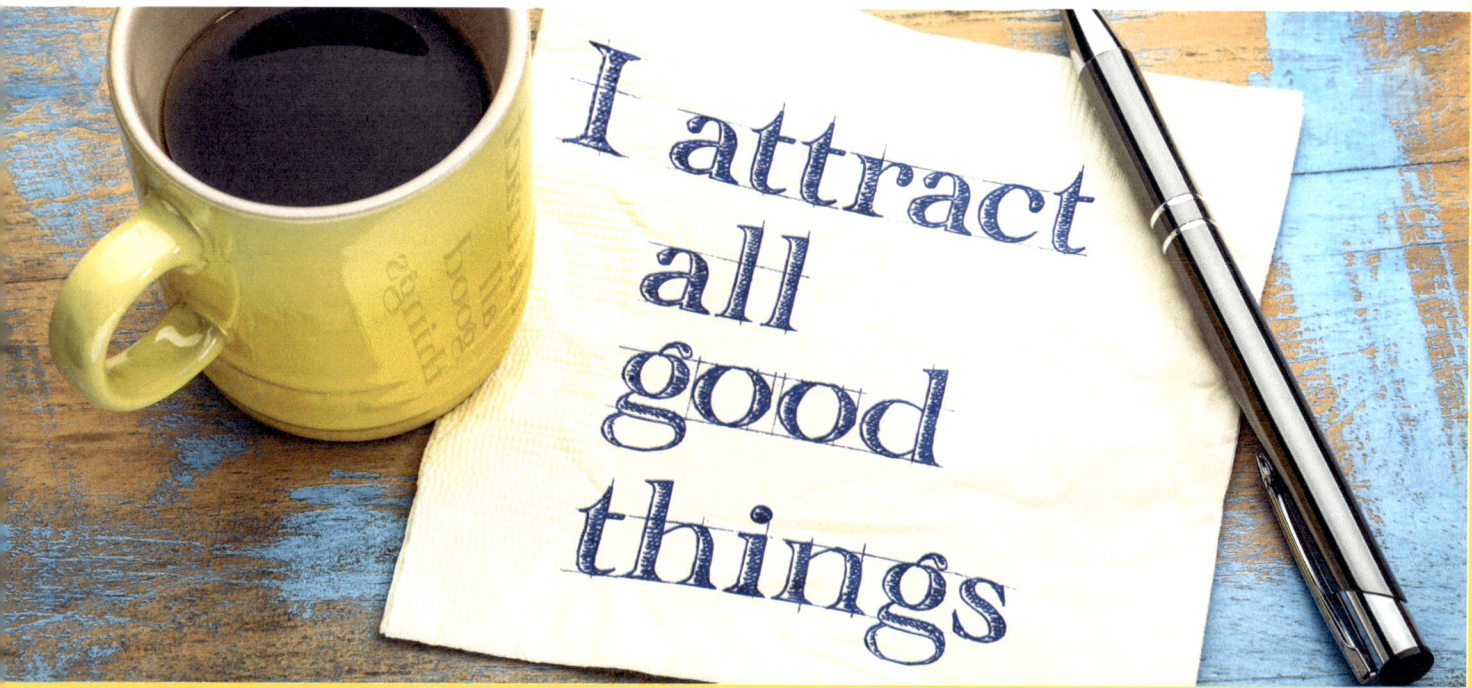

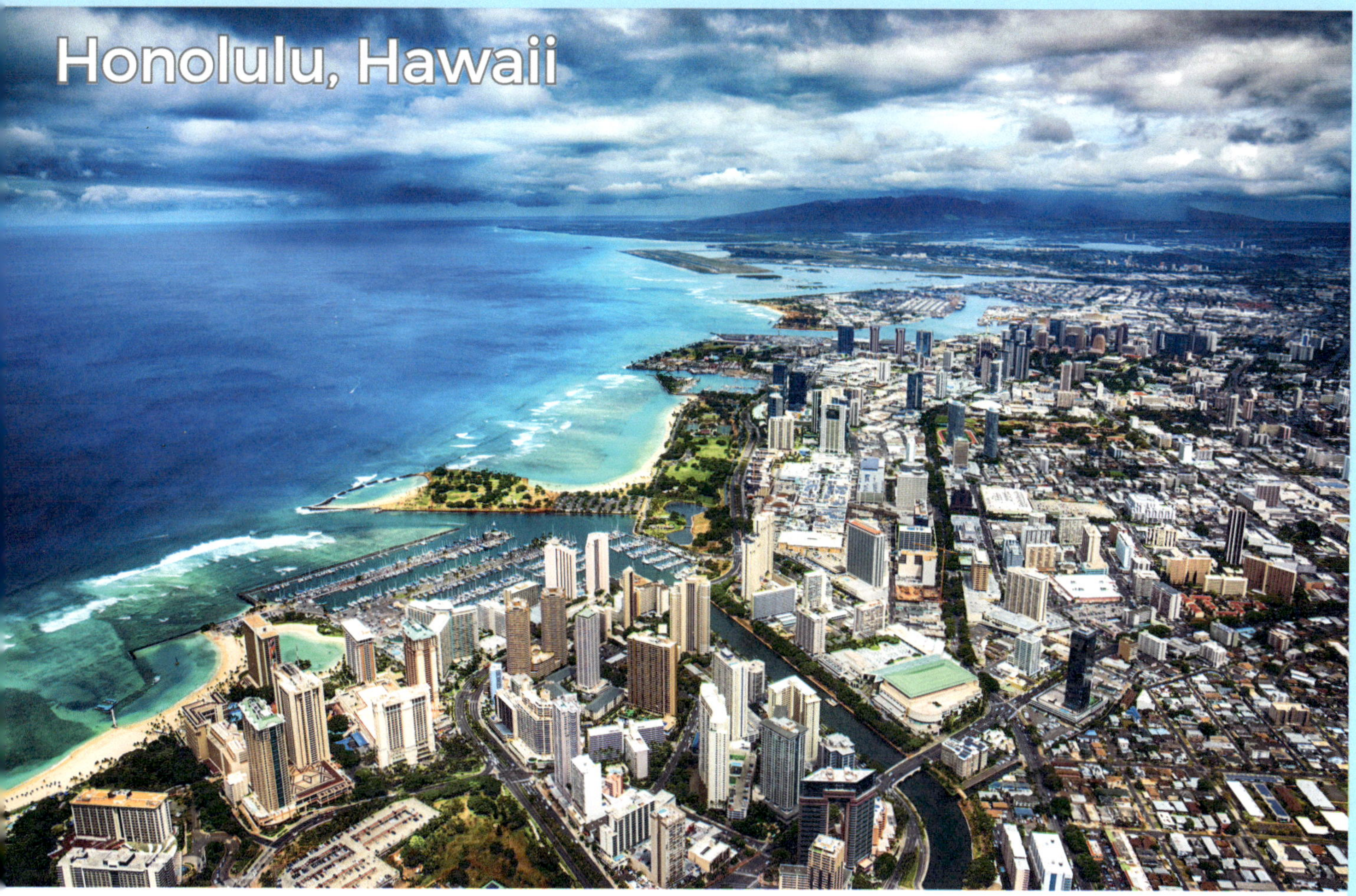

Honolulu, Hawaii

Tokyo, Japan

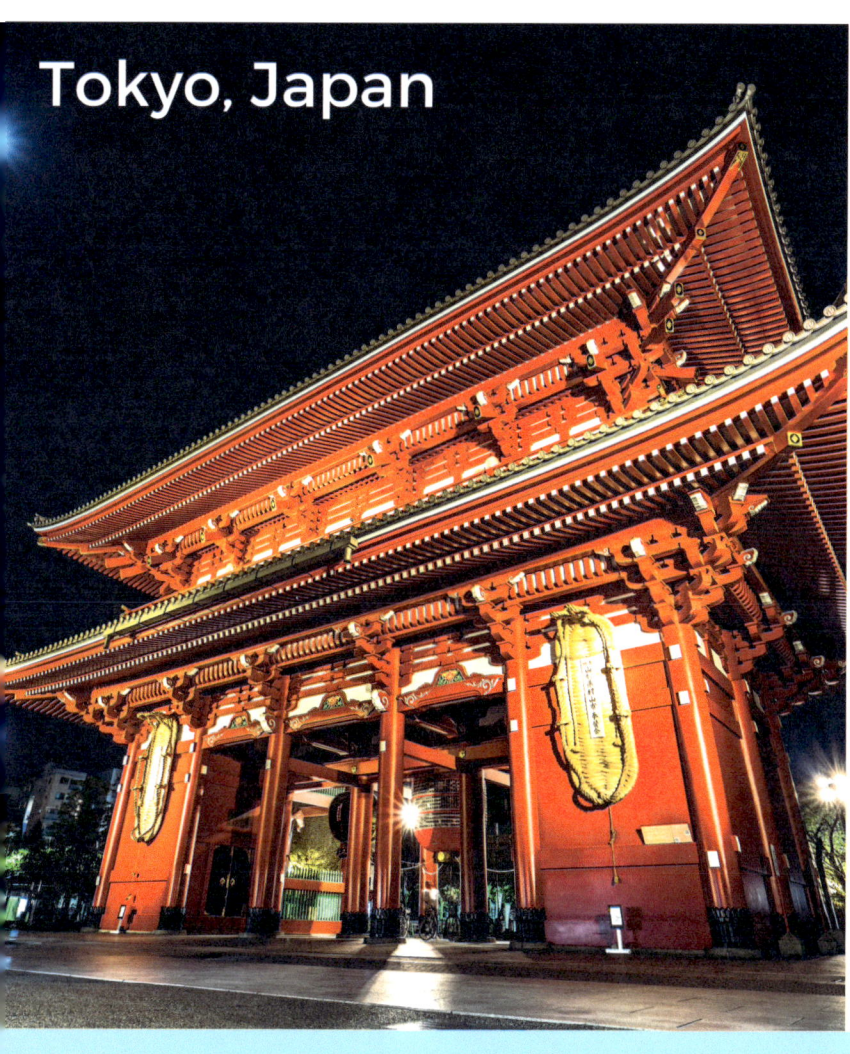

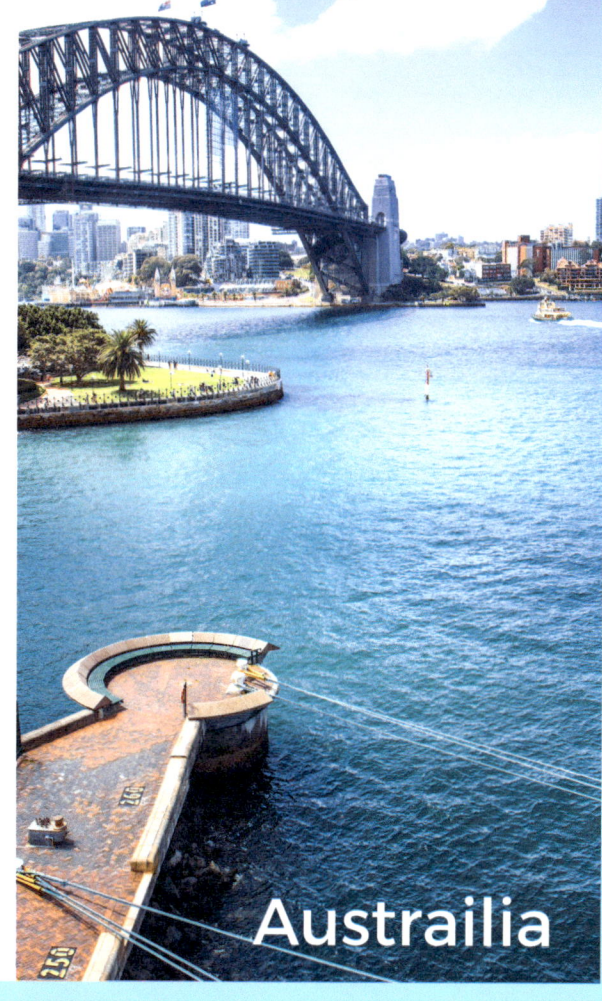

Austrailia

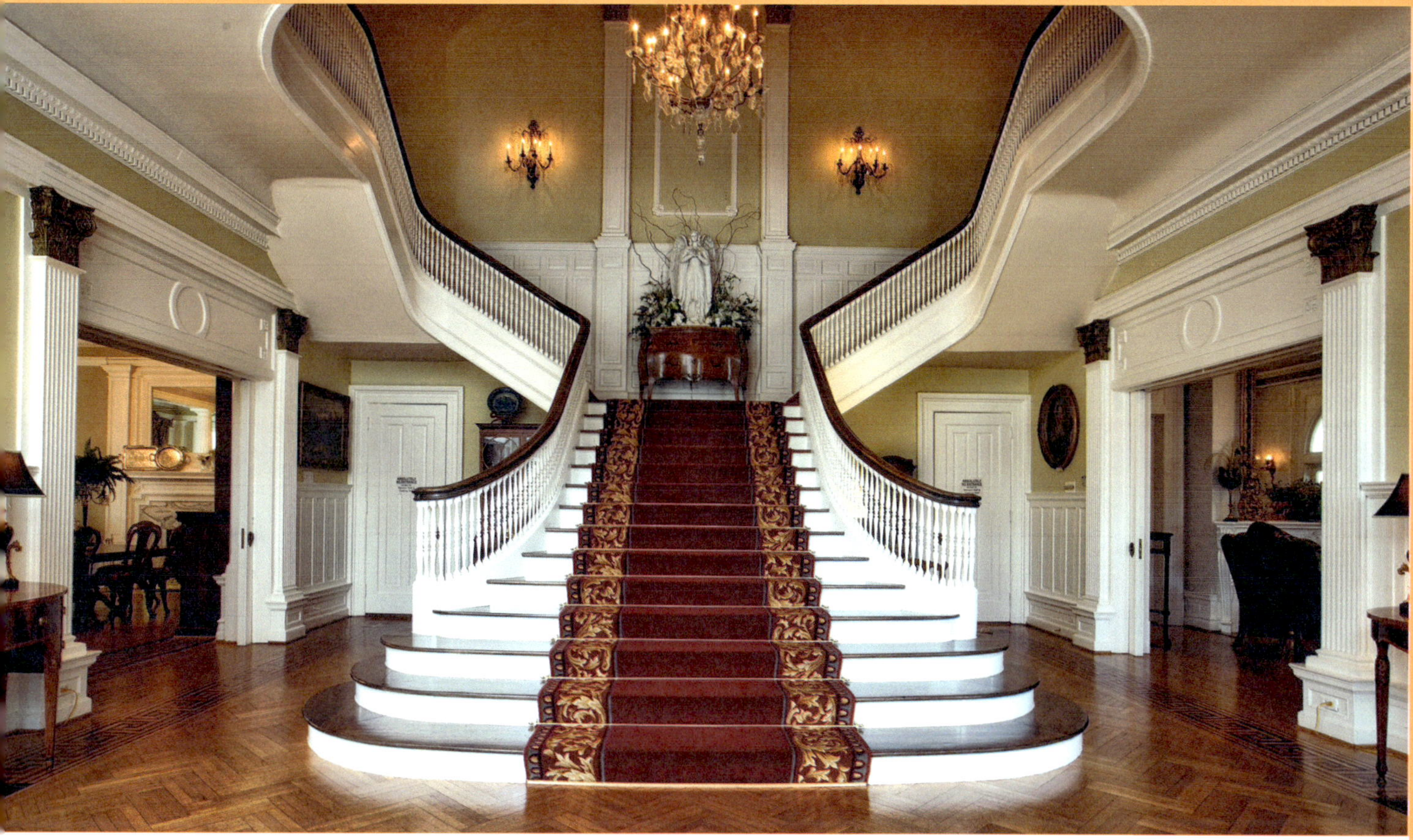

DREAM HOMES

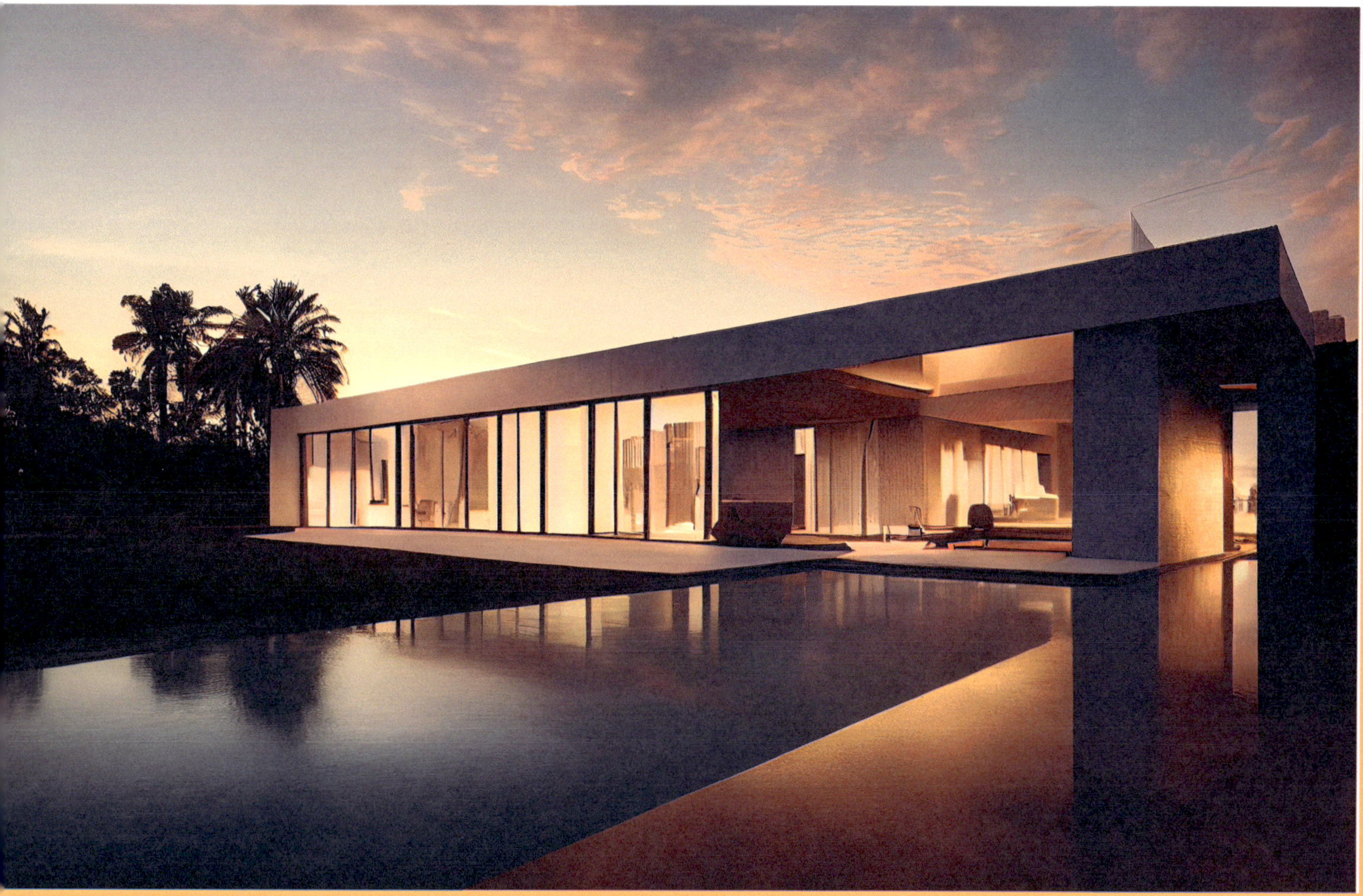

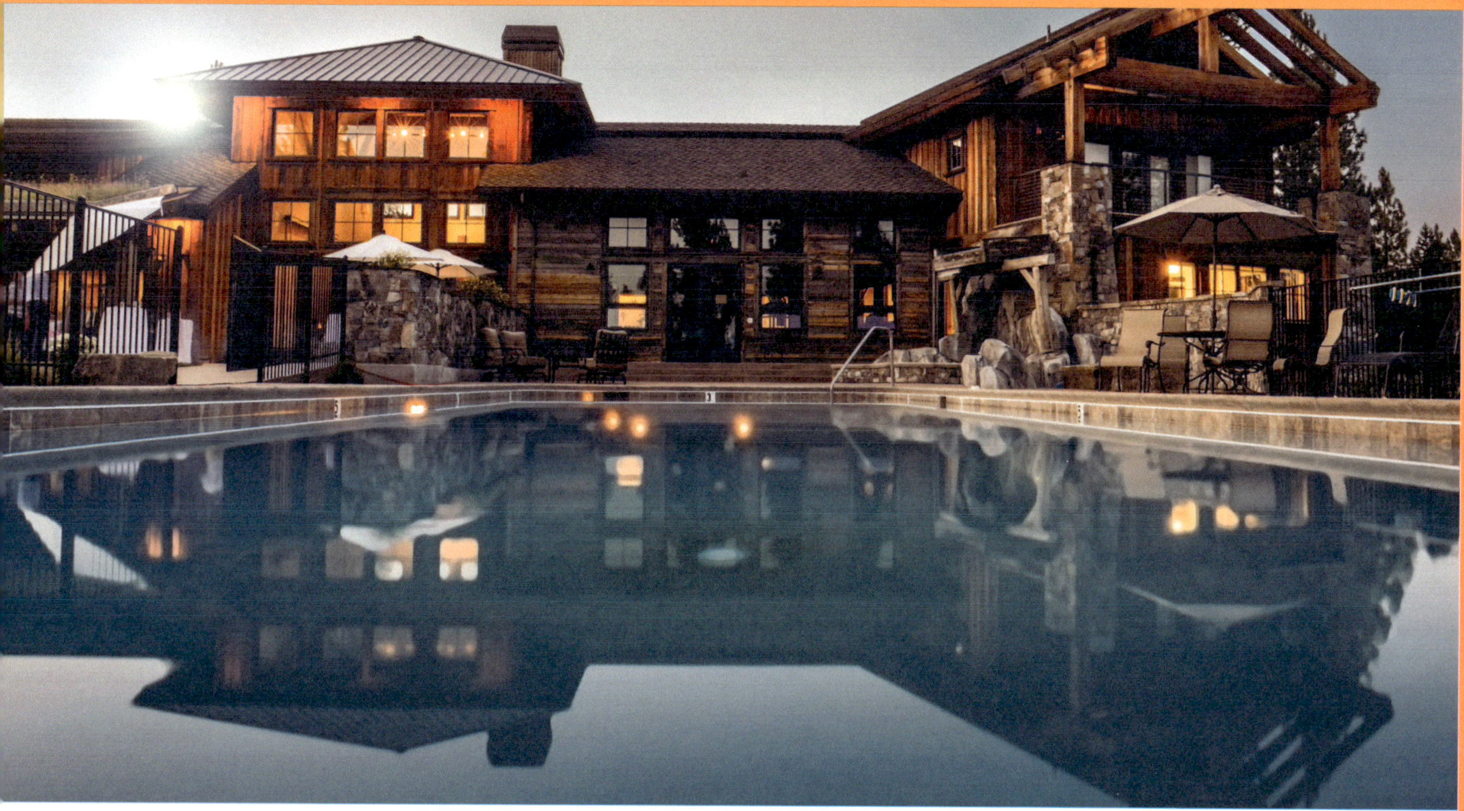

I am able to work hard to get the good things in life.

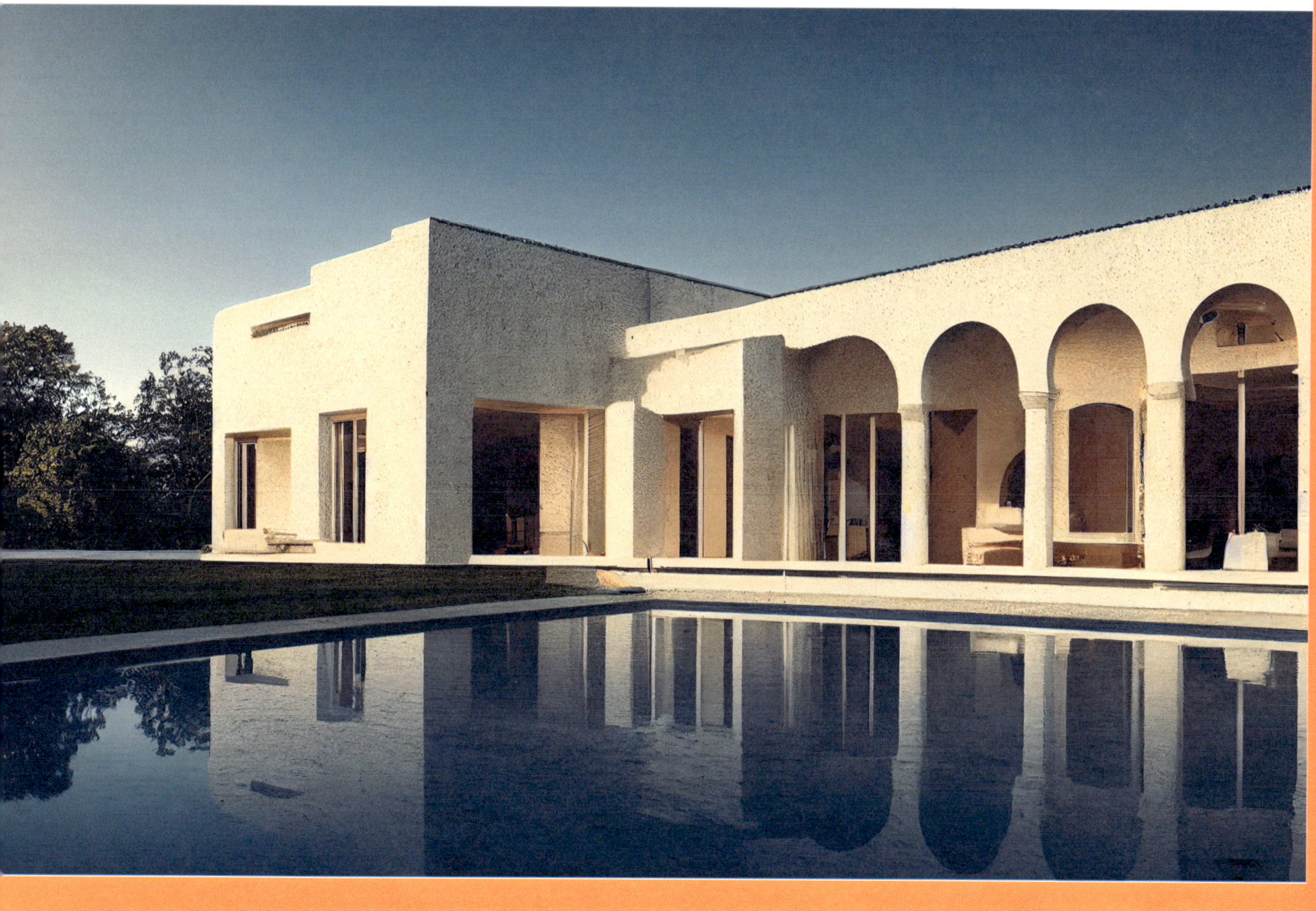

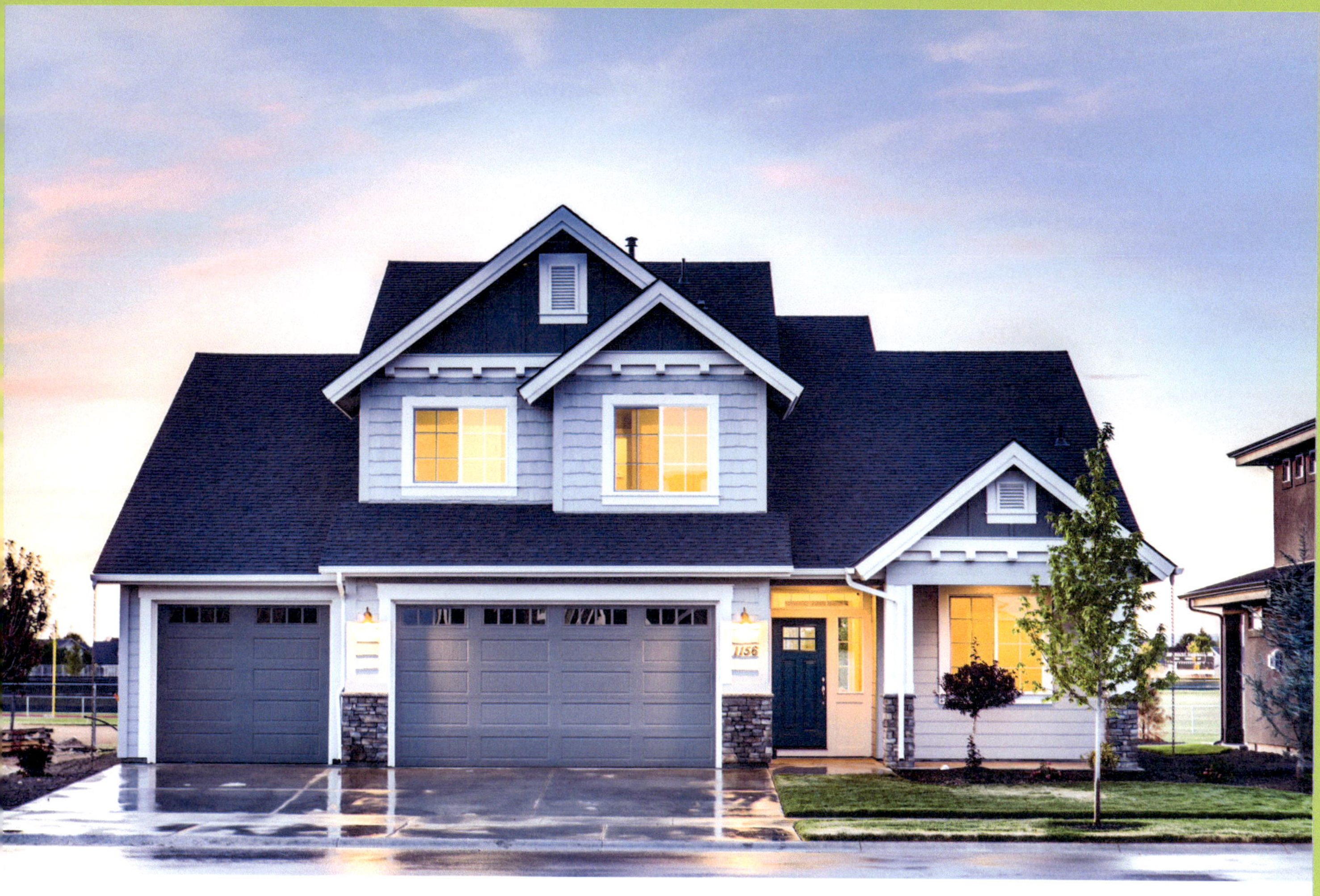

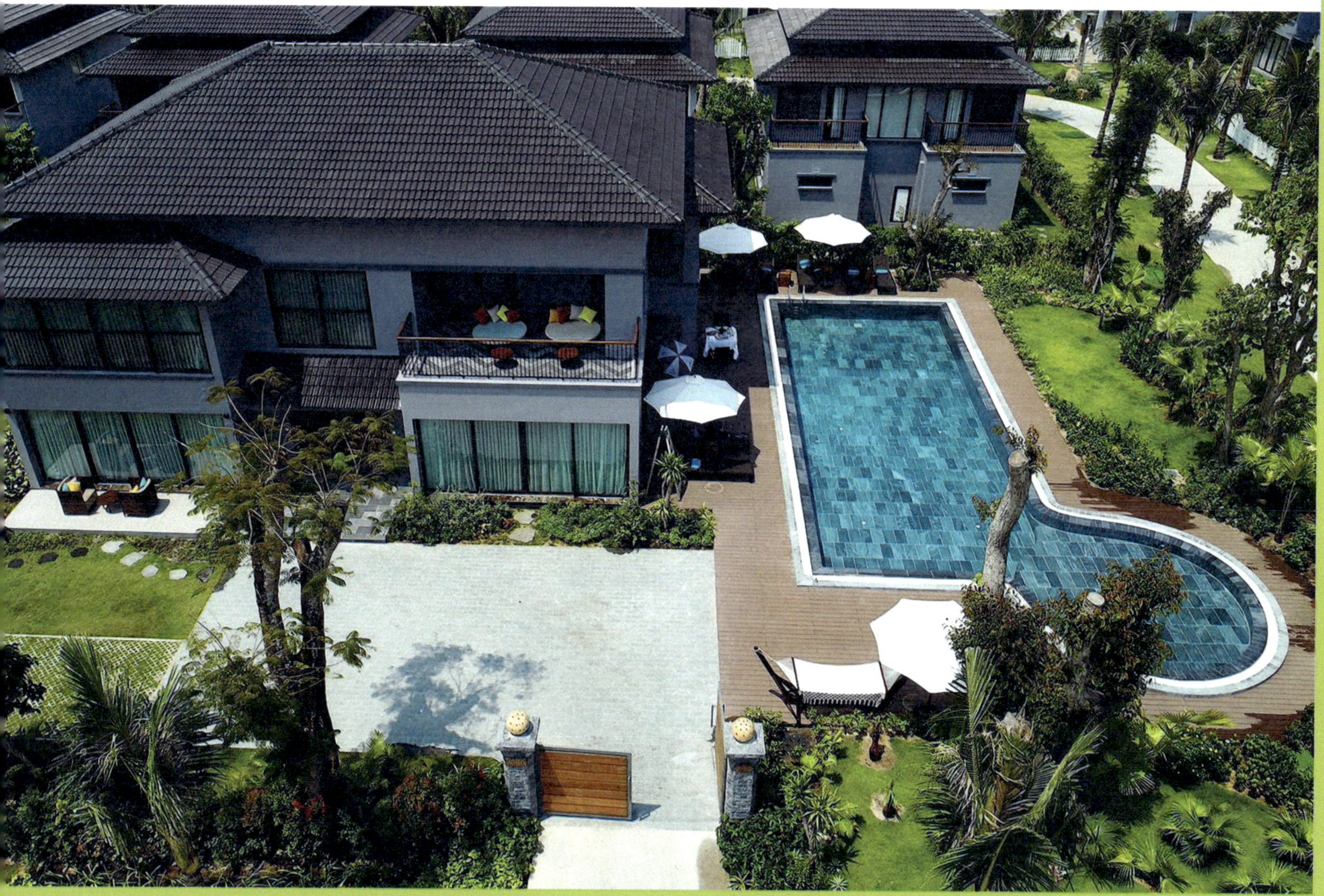

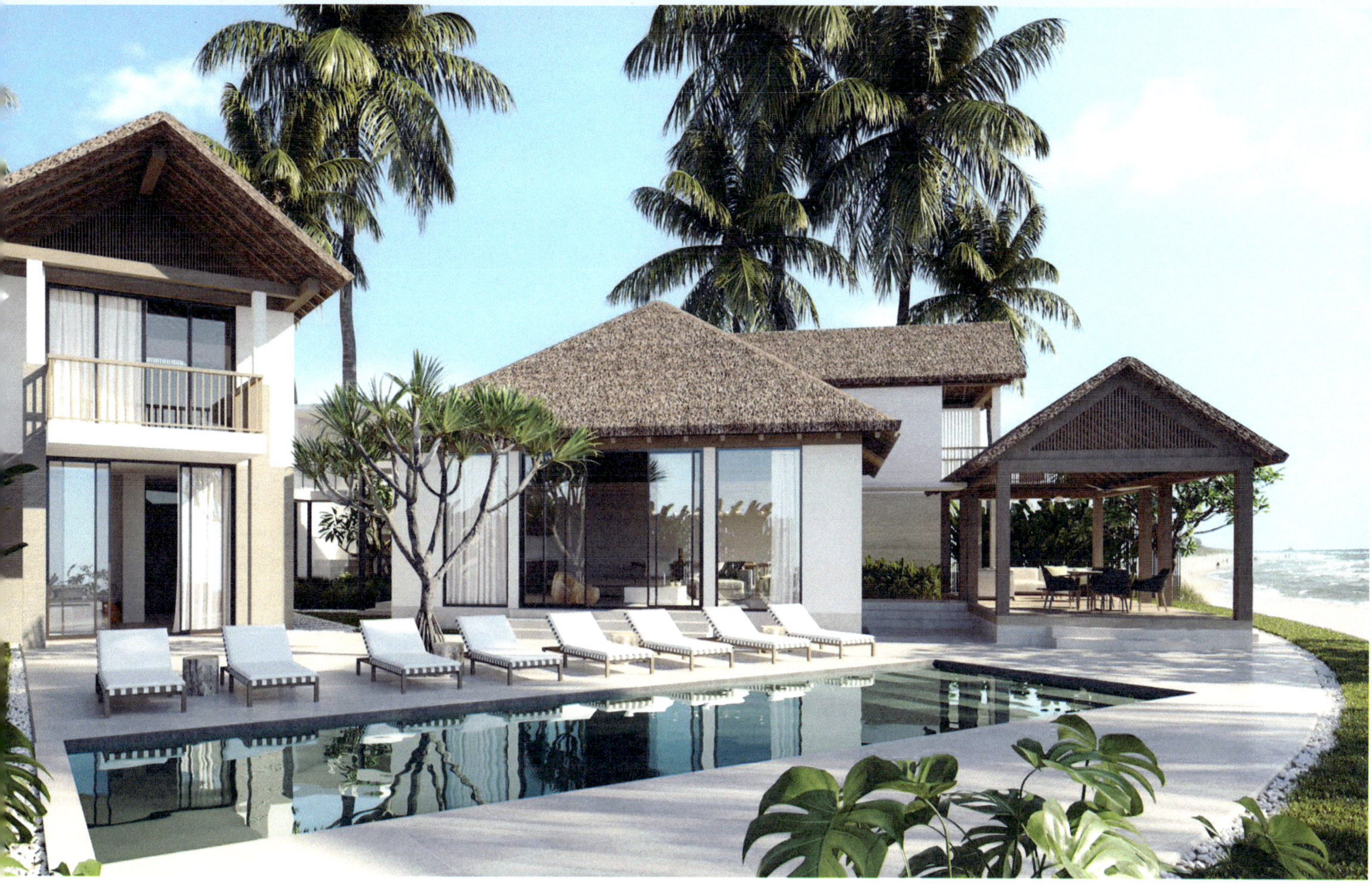

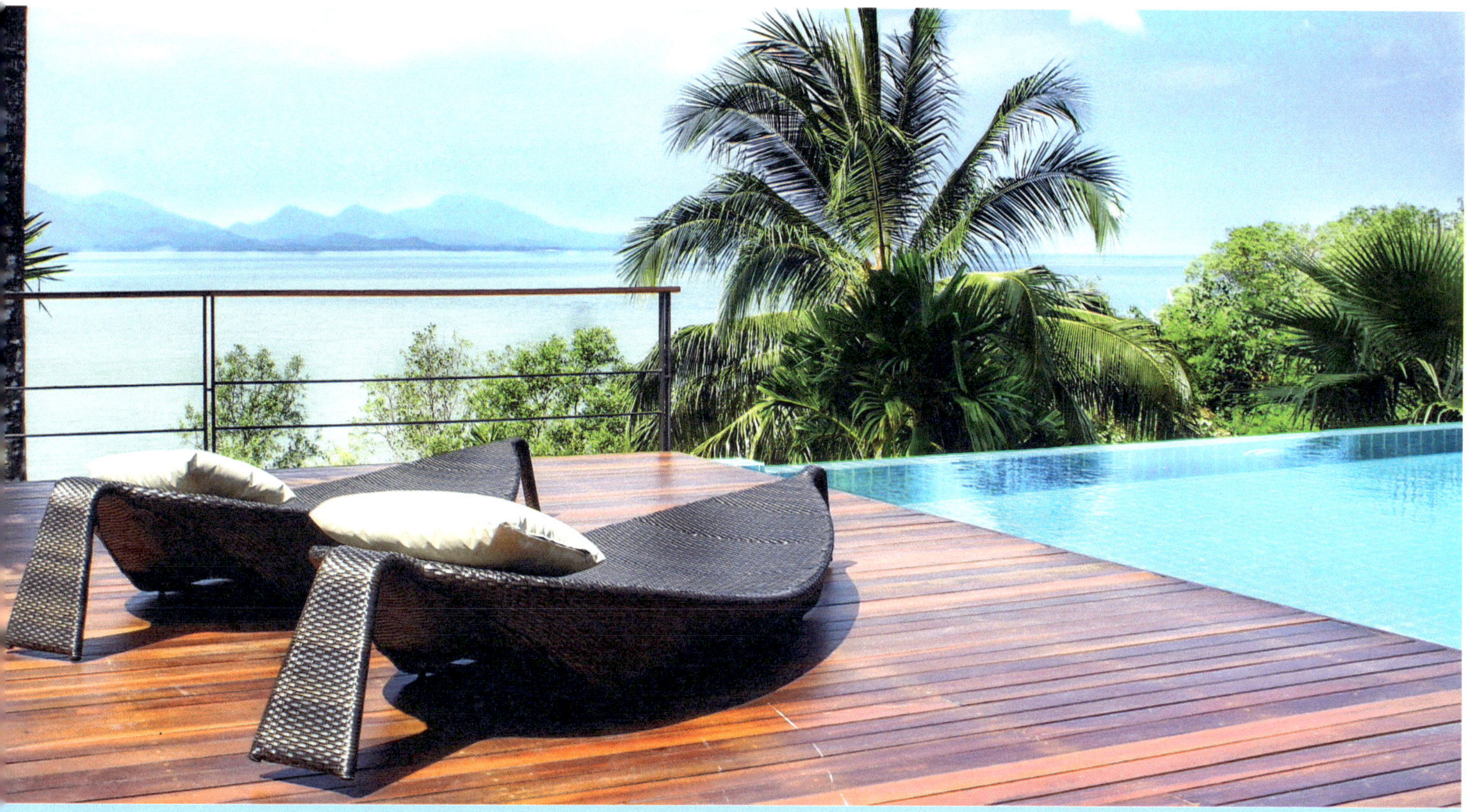

Dream Big, Achieve Luxuries.

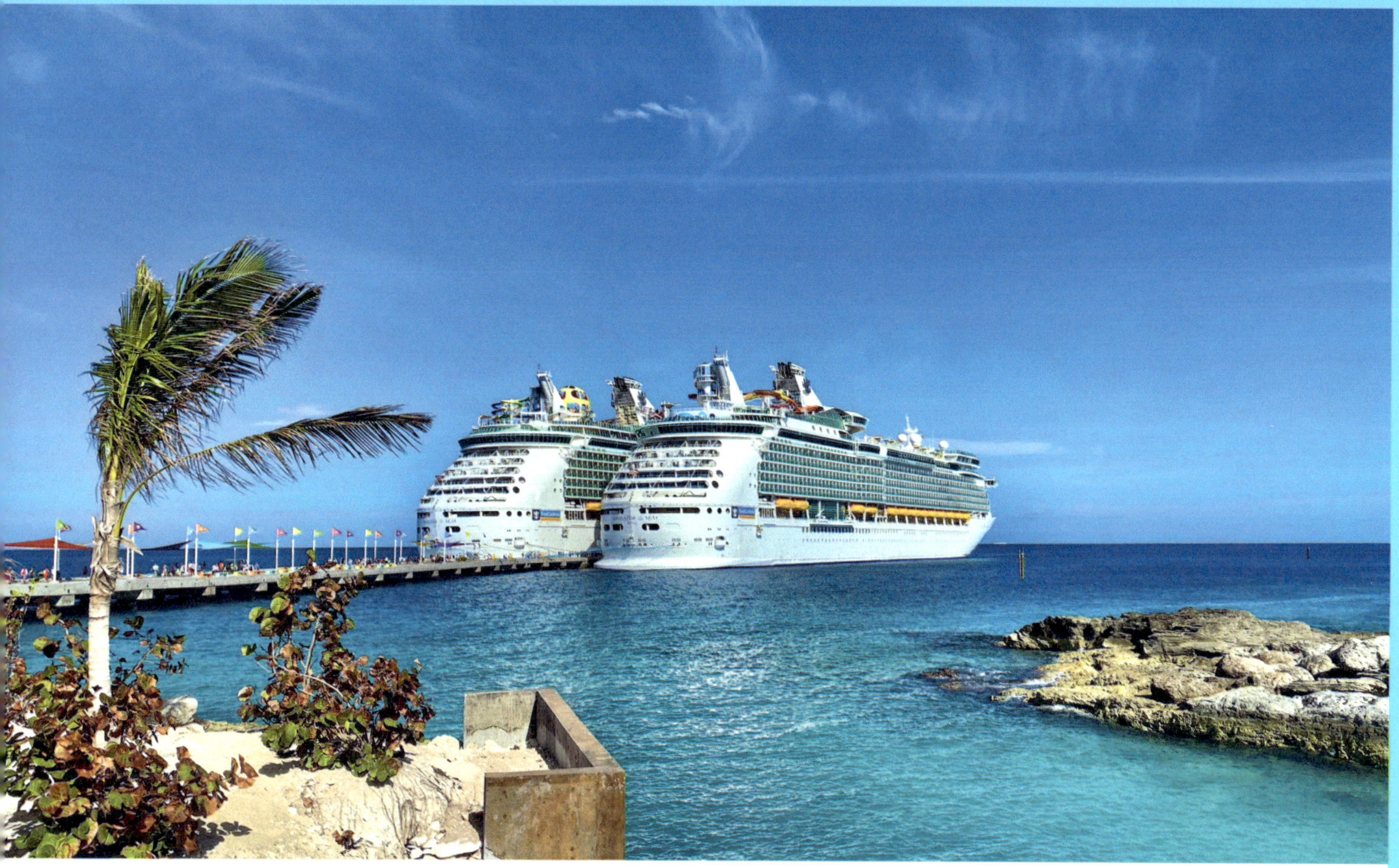

Luxury Liner ships and boats

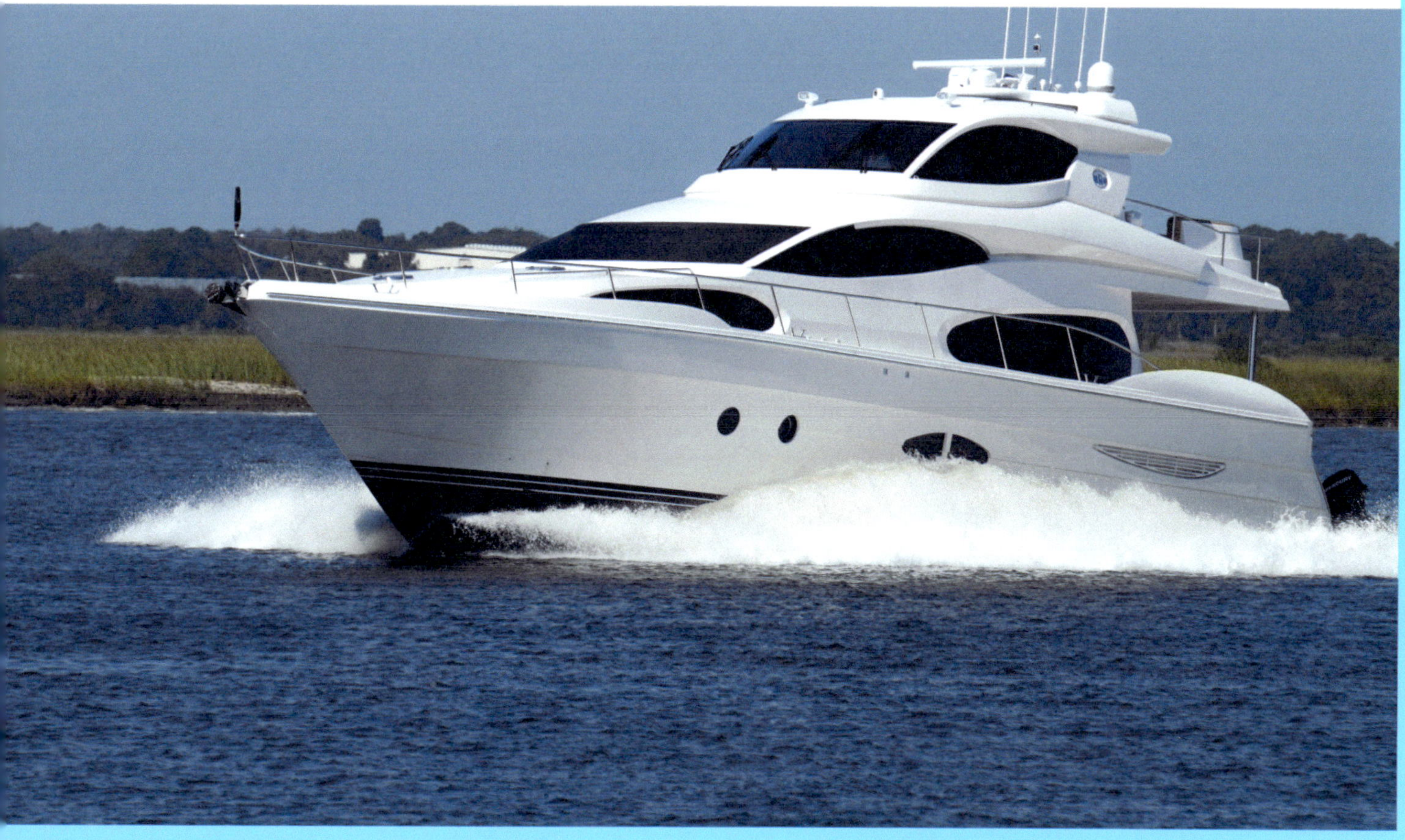

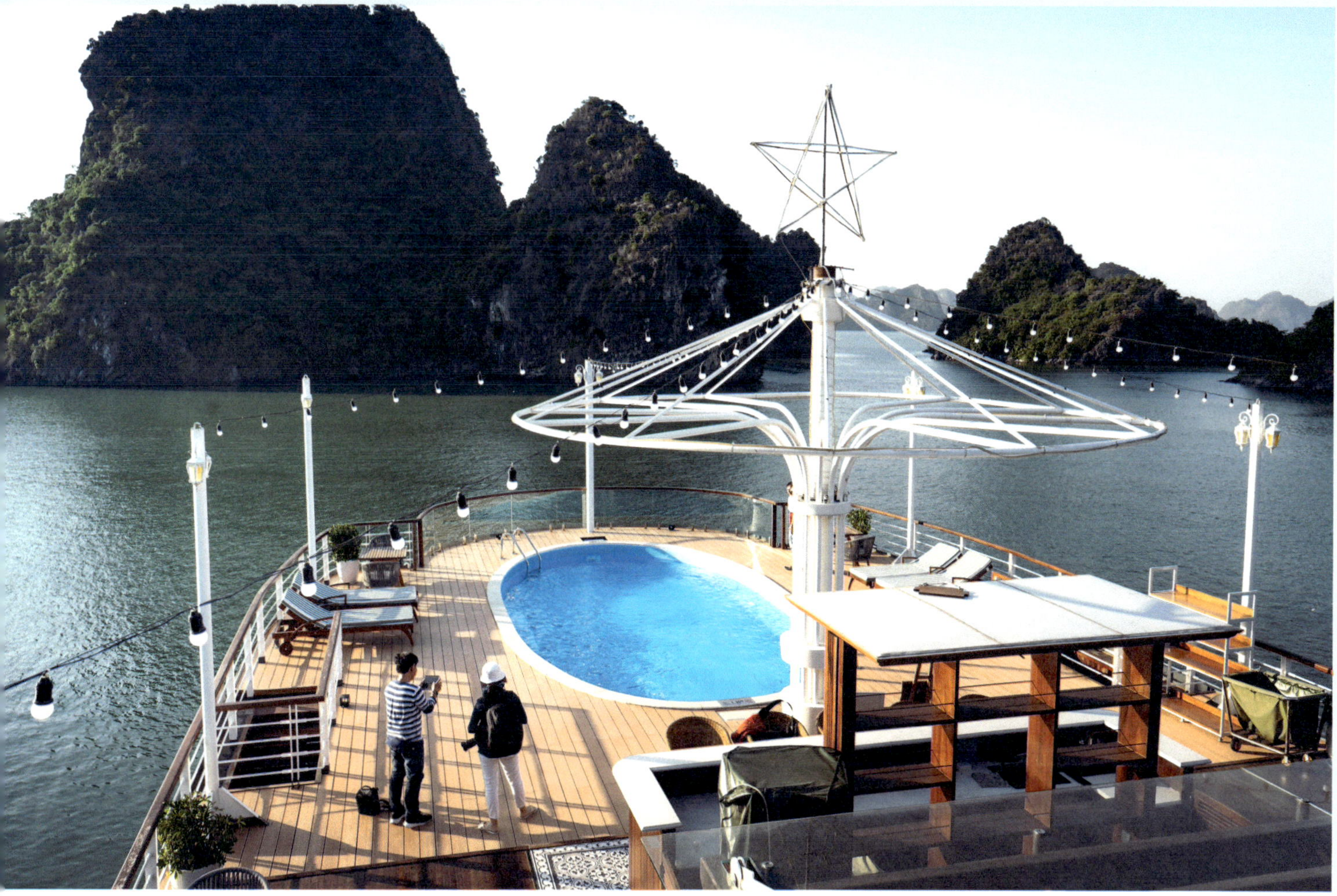

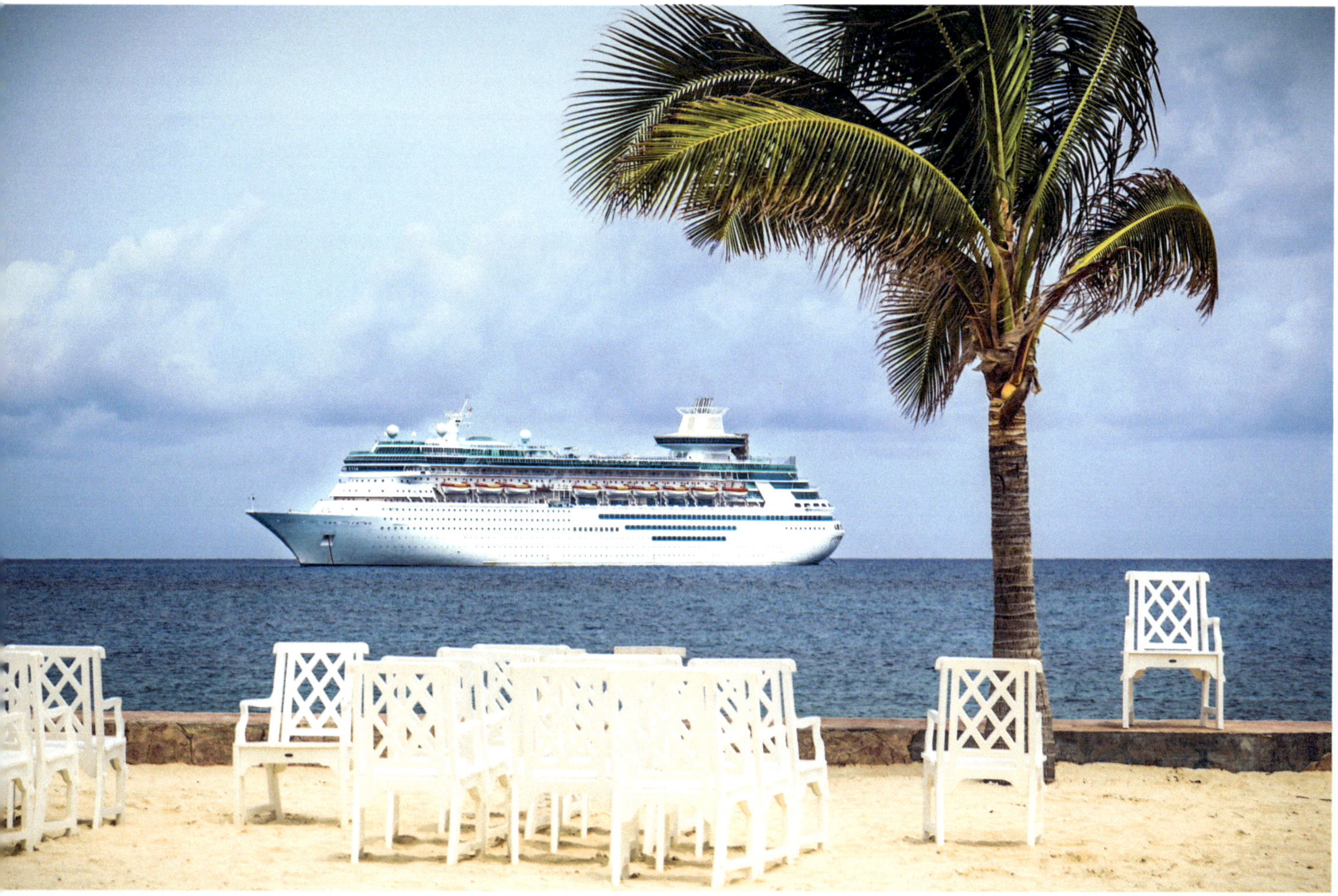

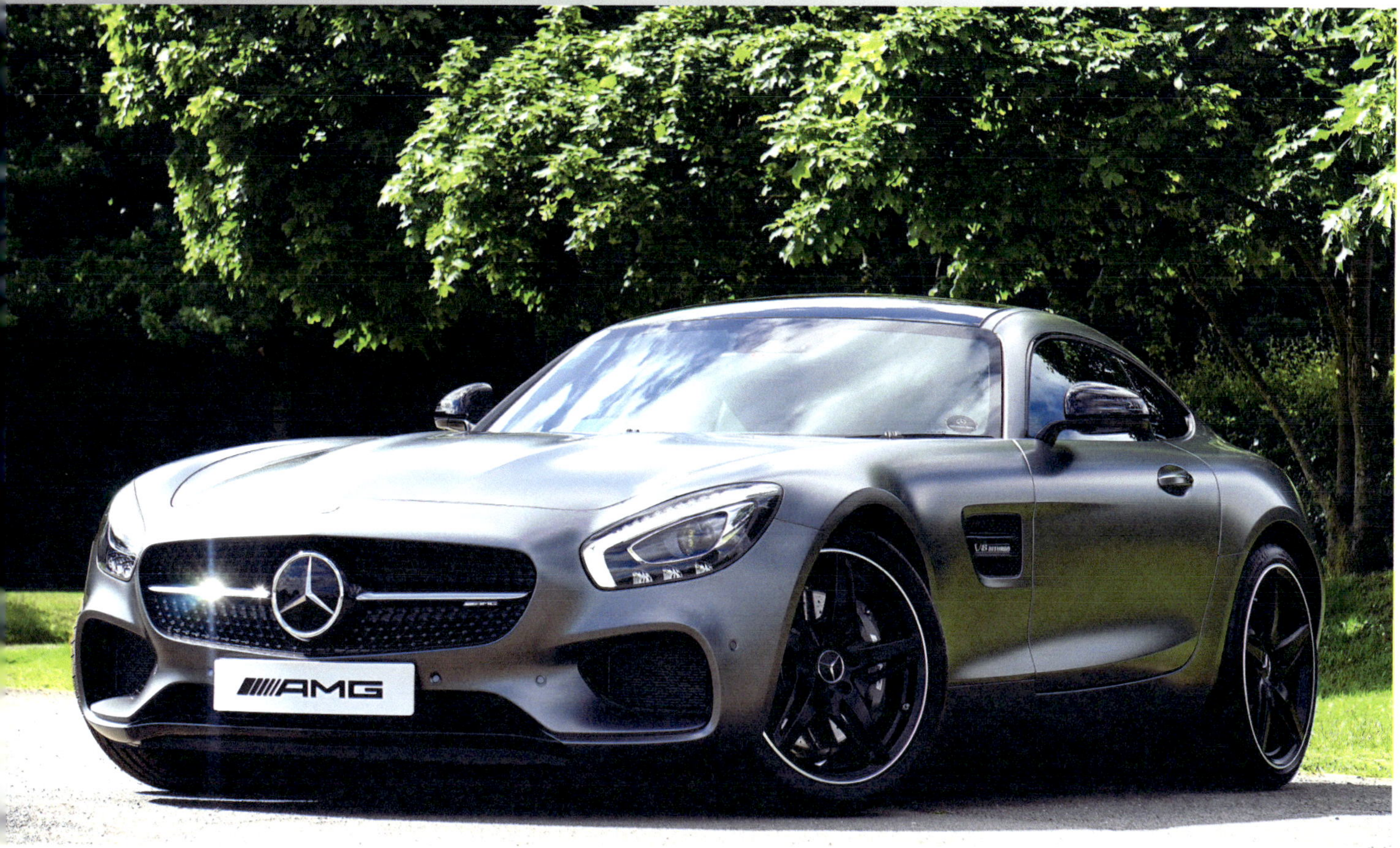

I am deserving of the luxuries of life.

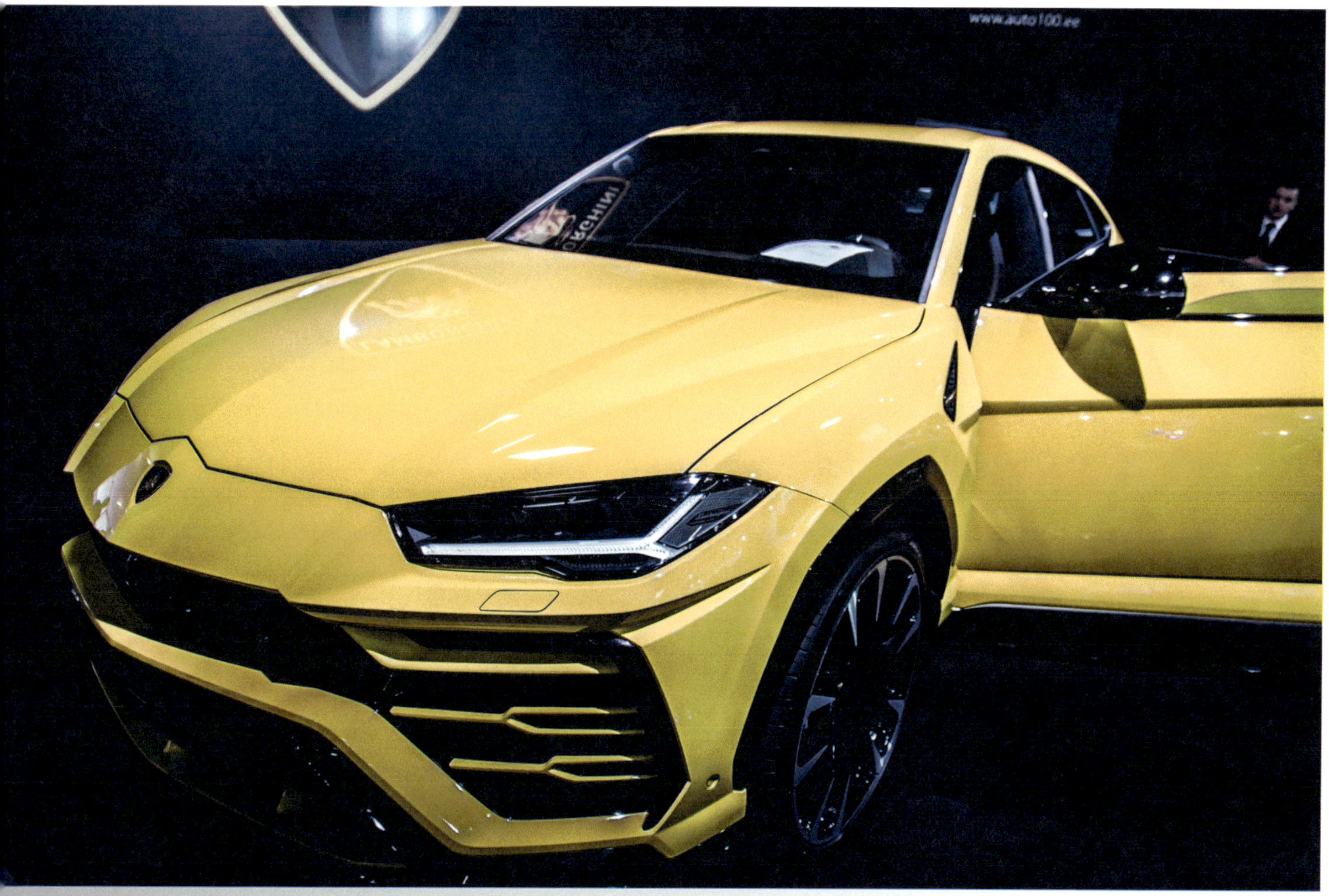

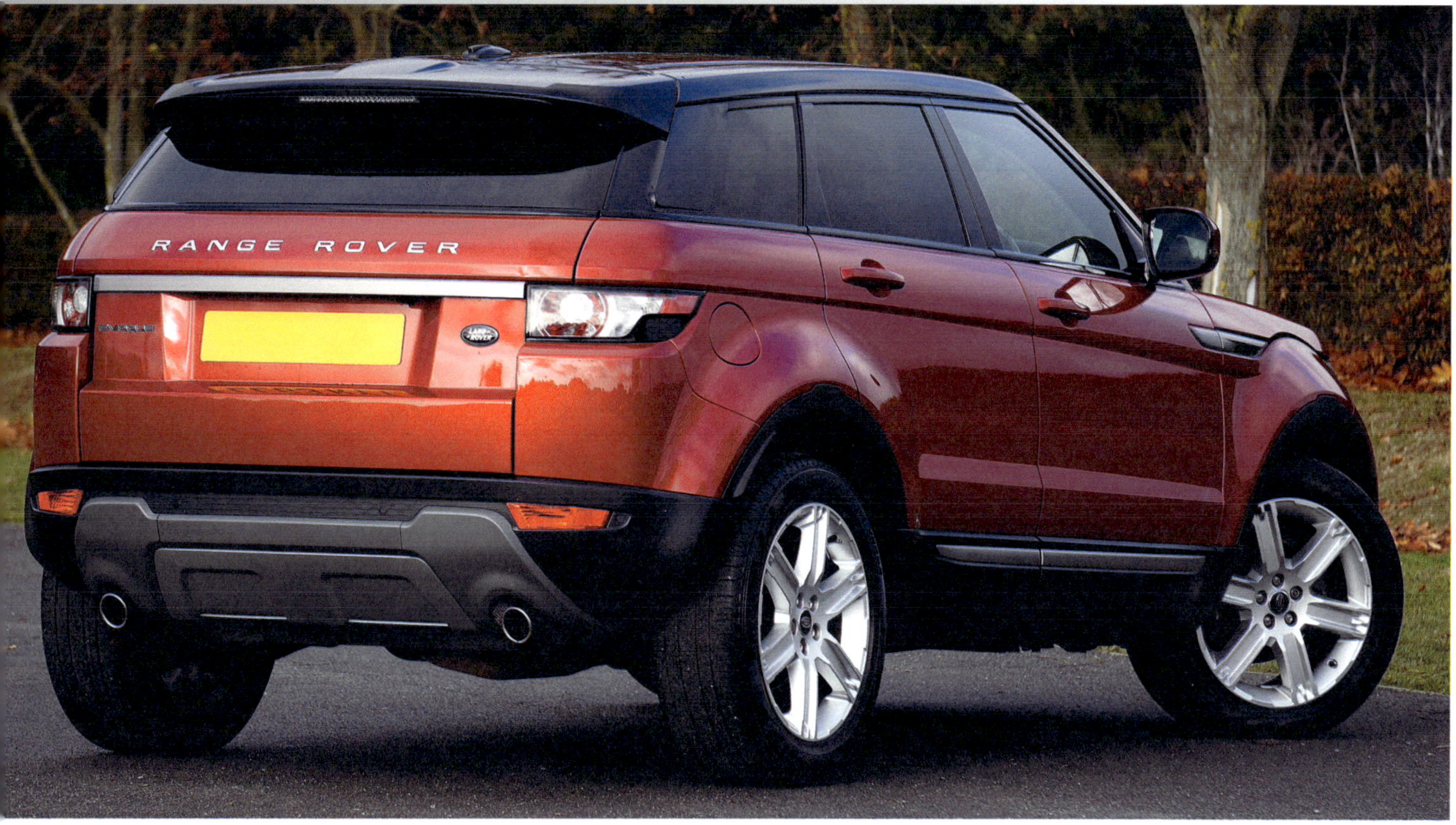

I am capable of achieving my goals and living my dreams.

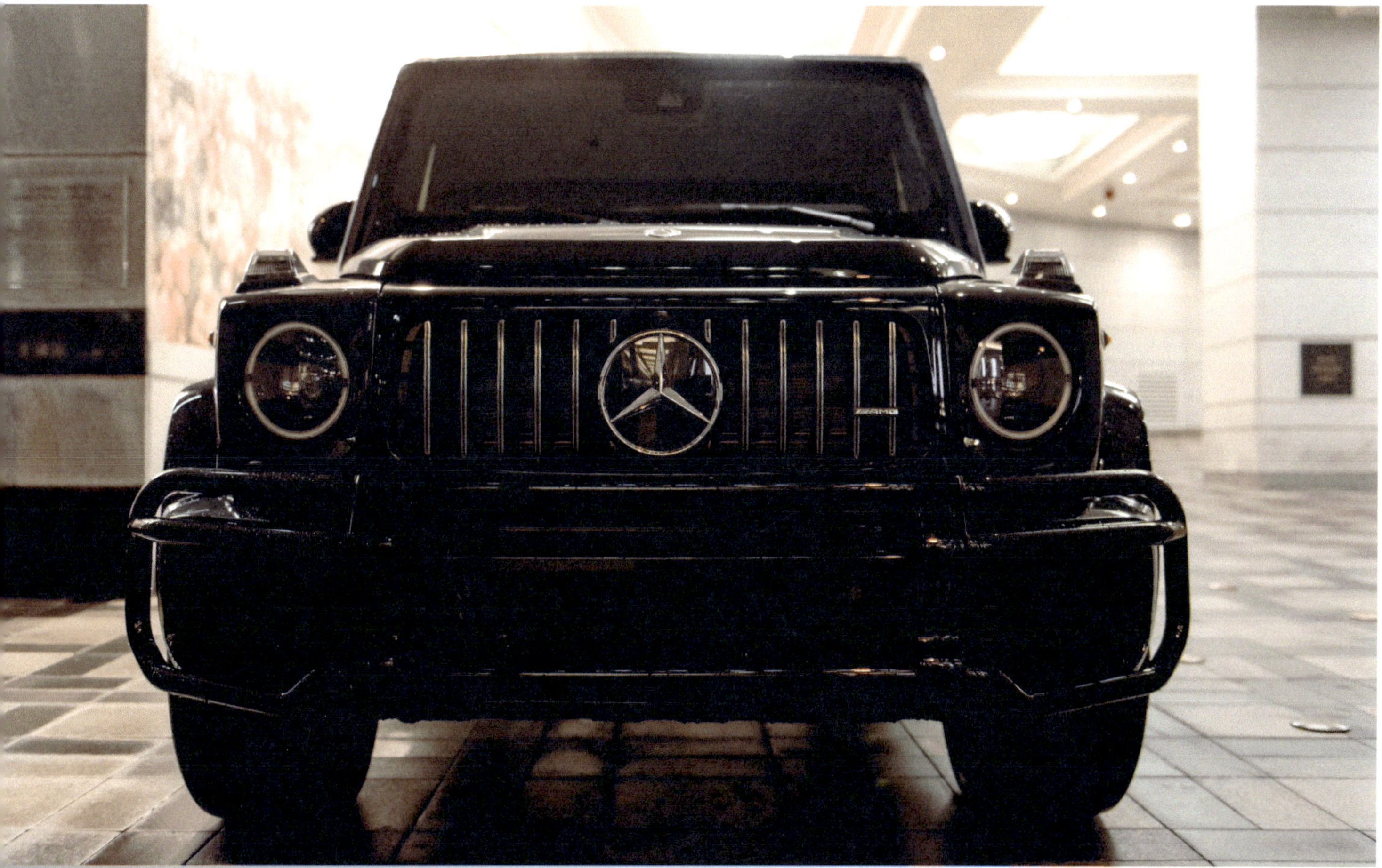

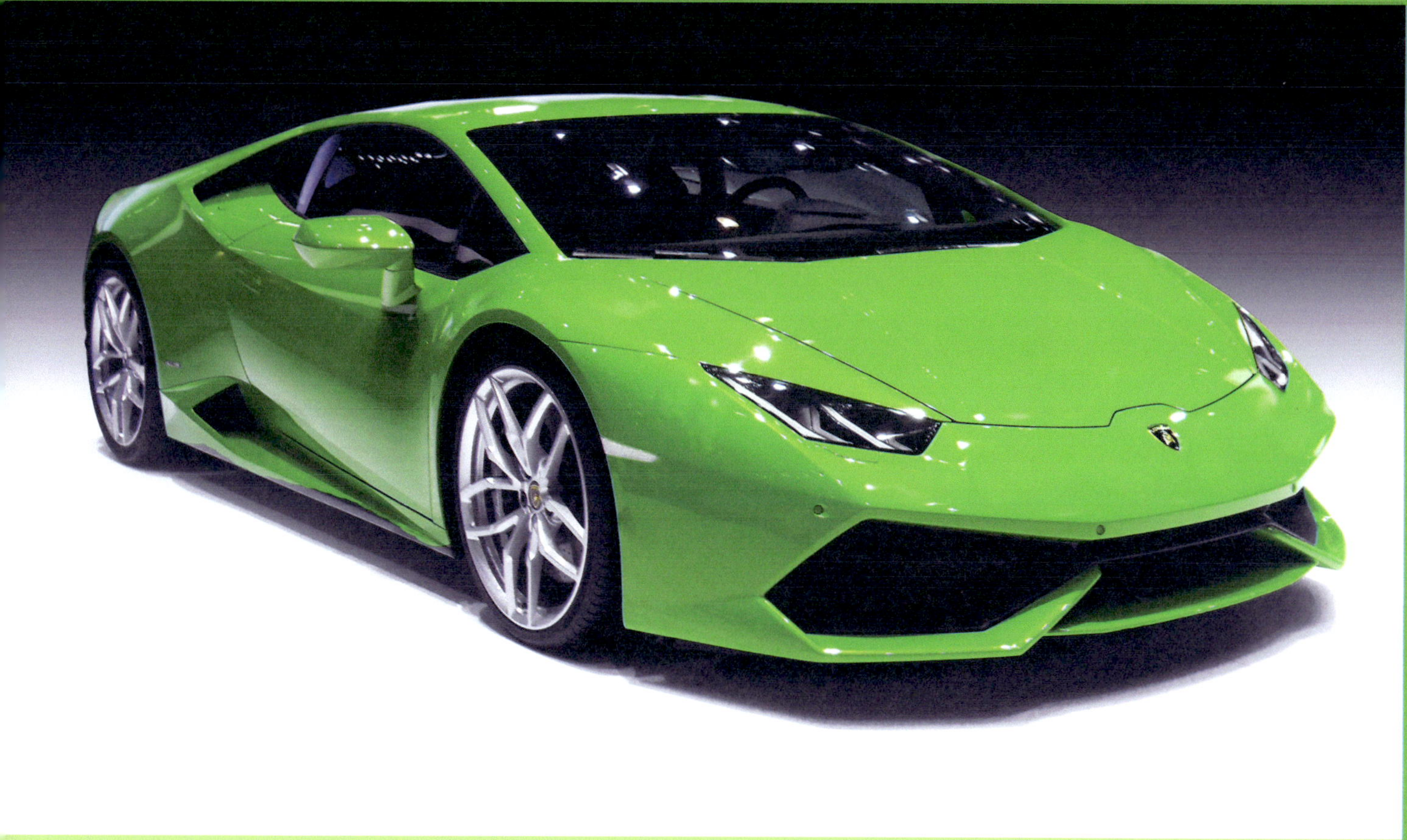

I am capable of manifesting my dreams and desires.

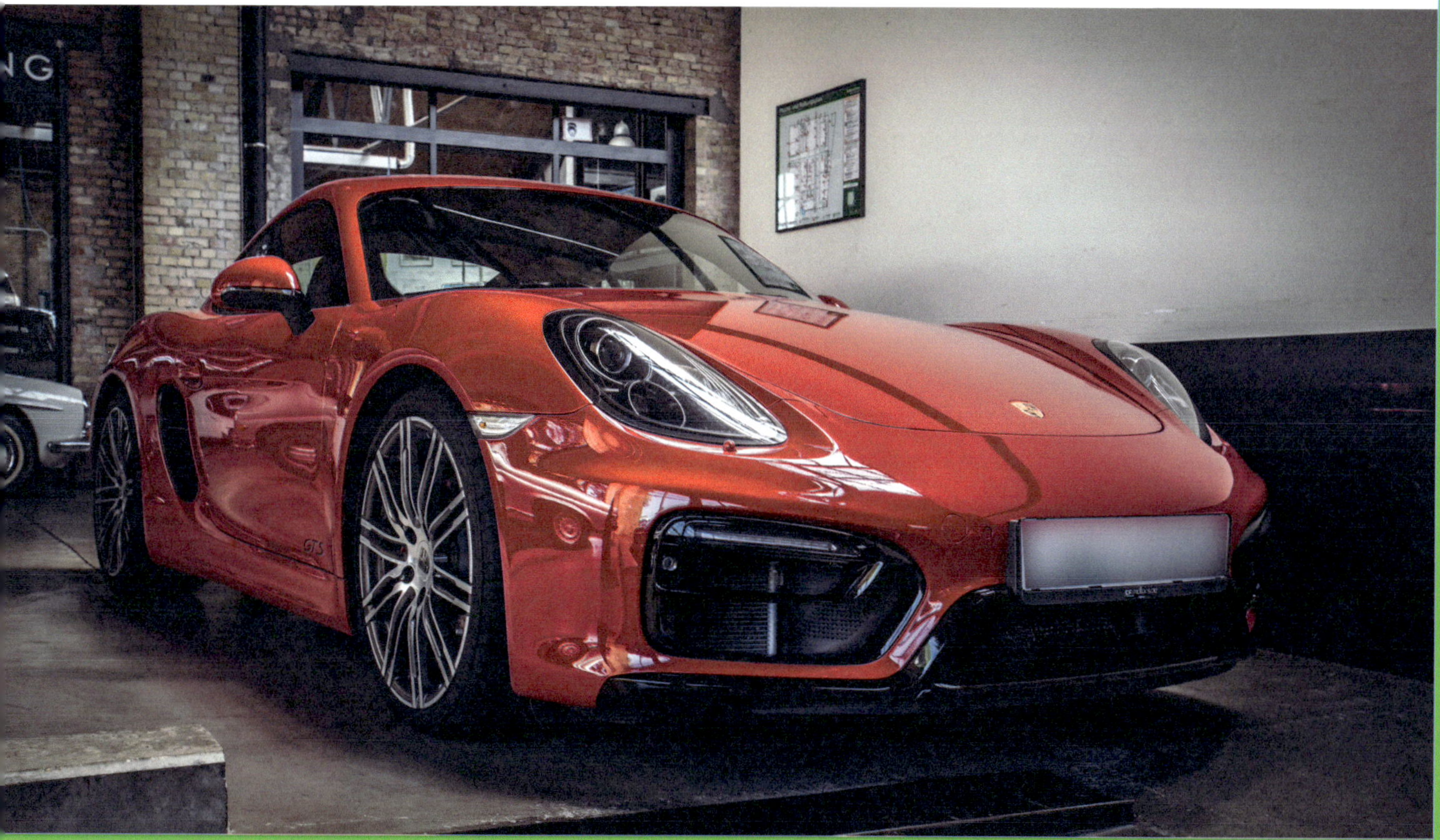

I am deserving of a life that is full of abundance, and prosperity.

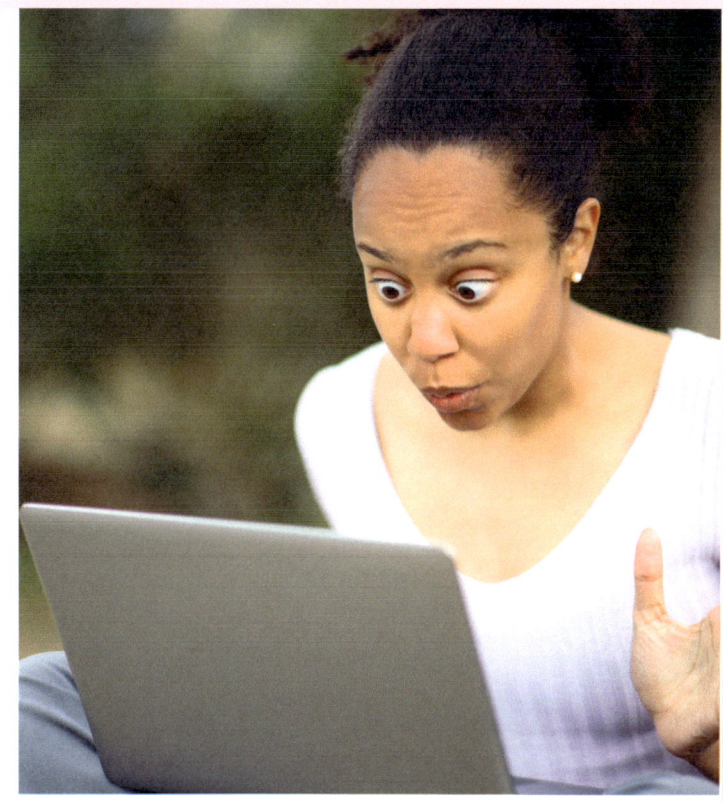
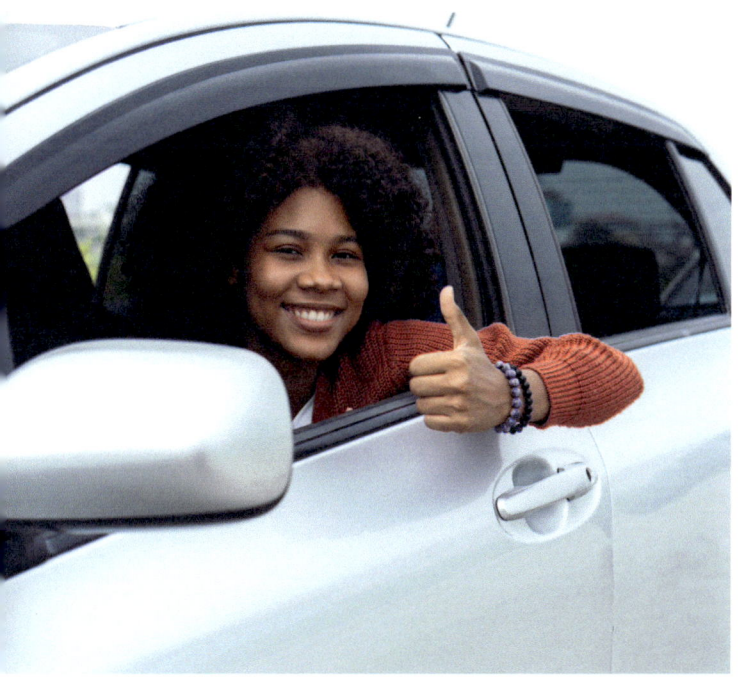
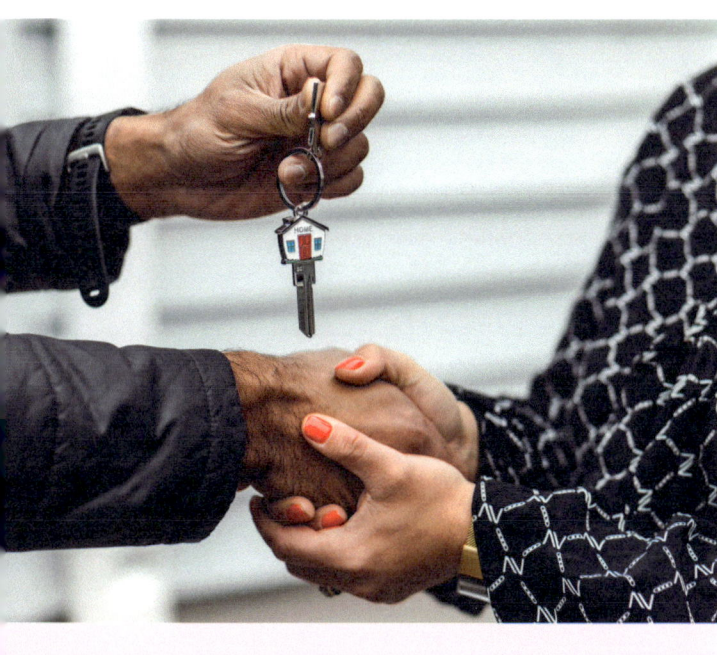
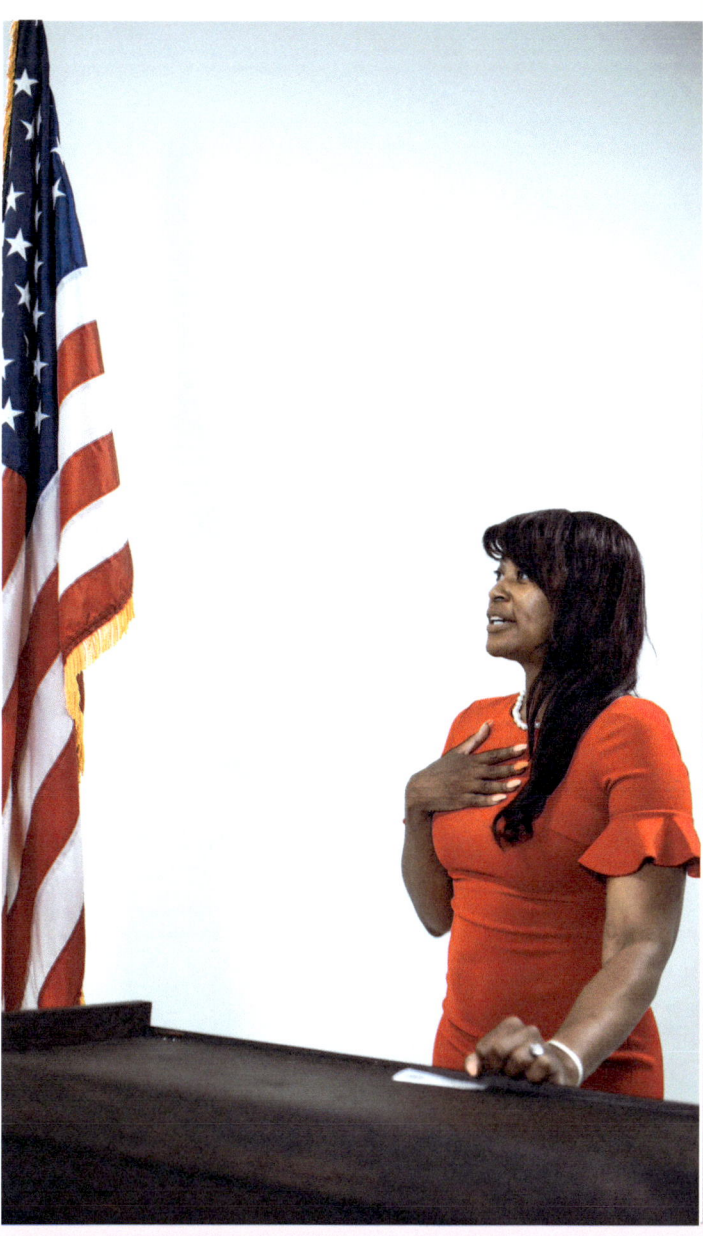

Learn More, Achieve More.

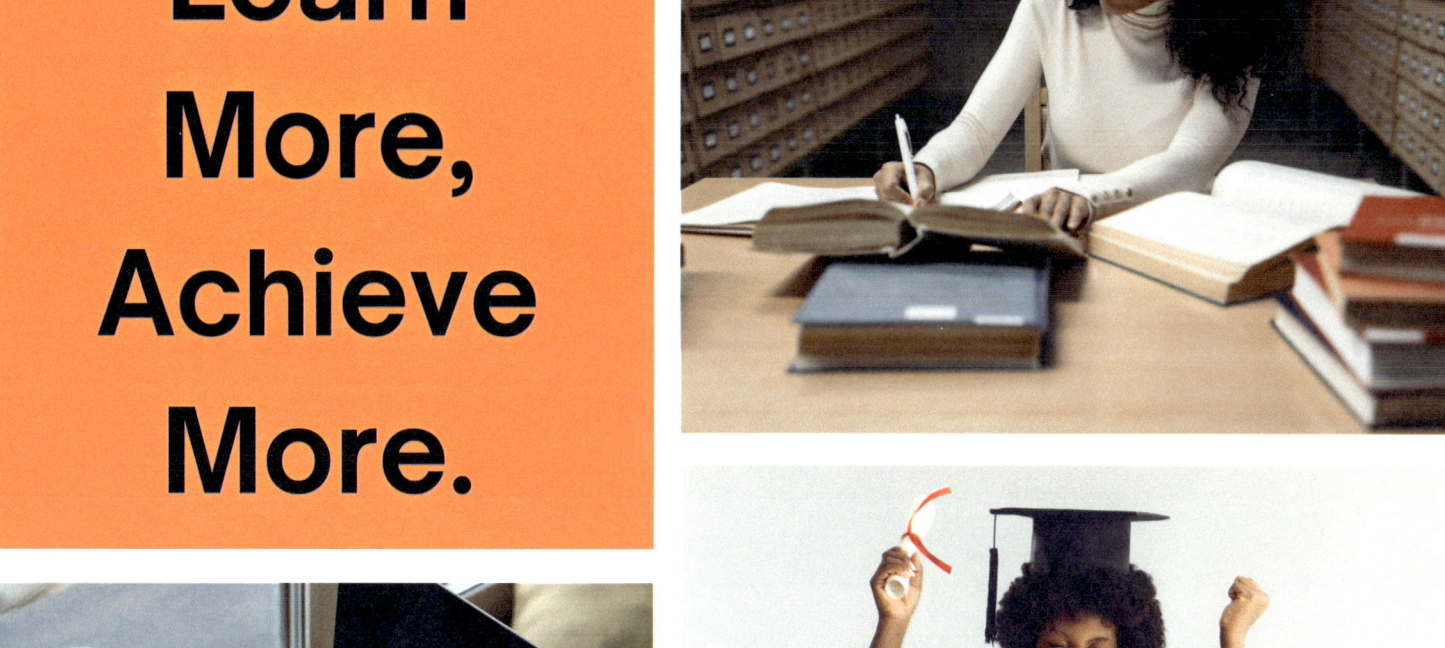
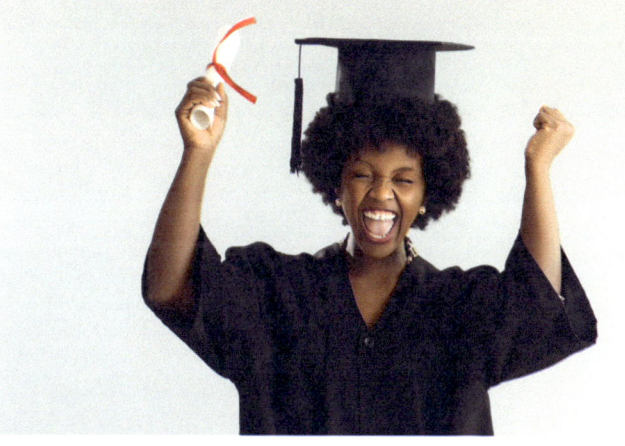
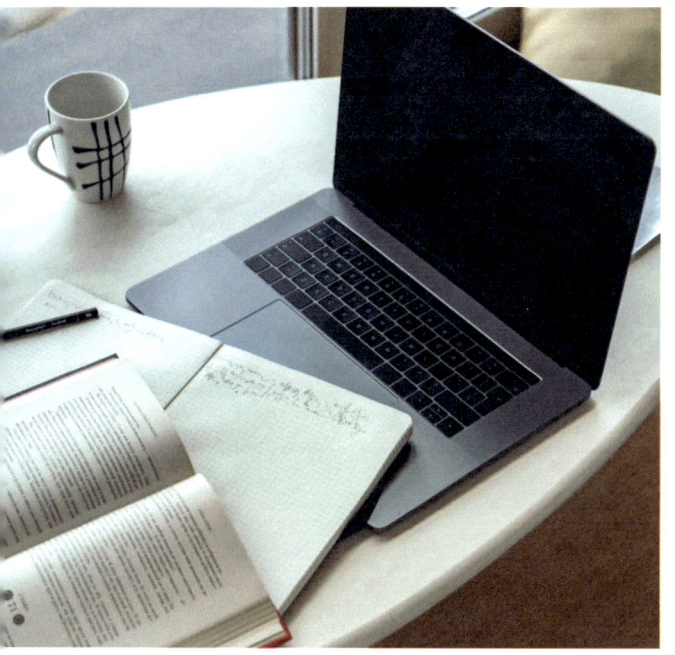
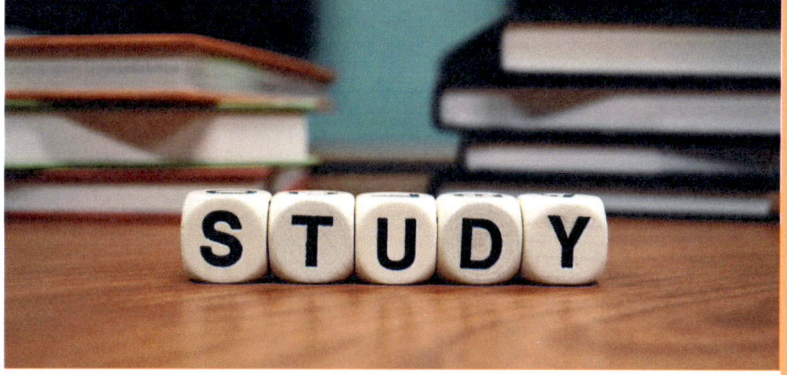
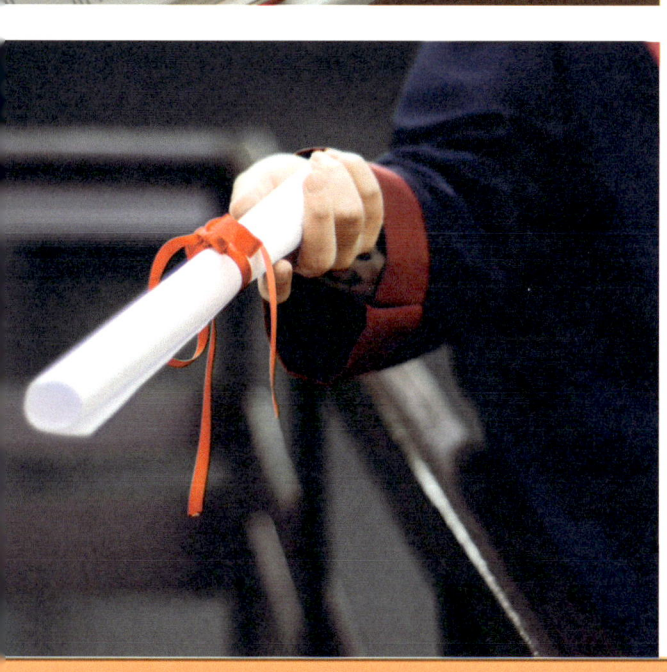
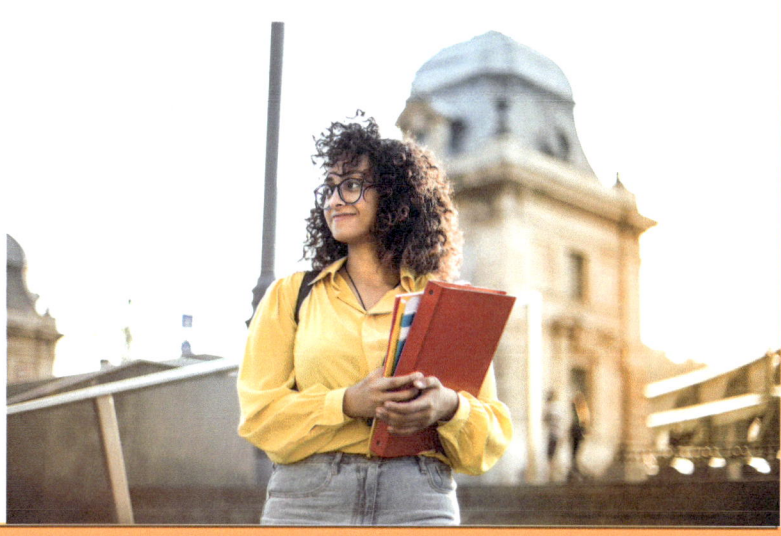

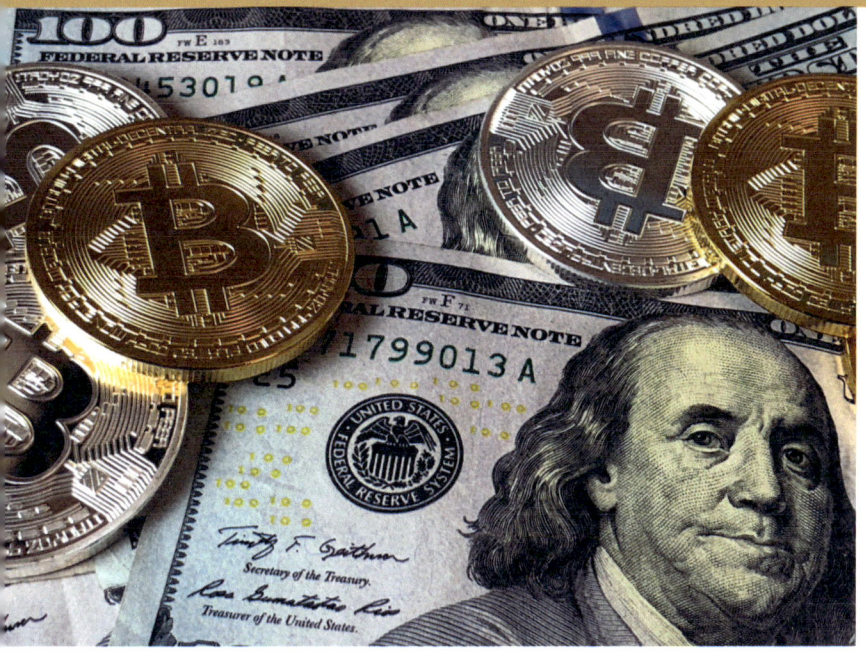
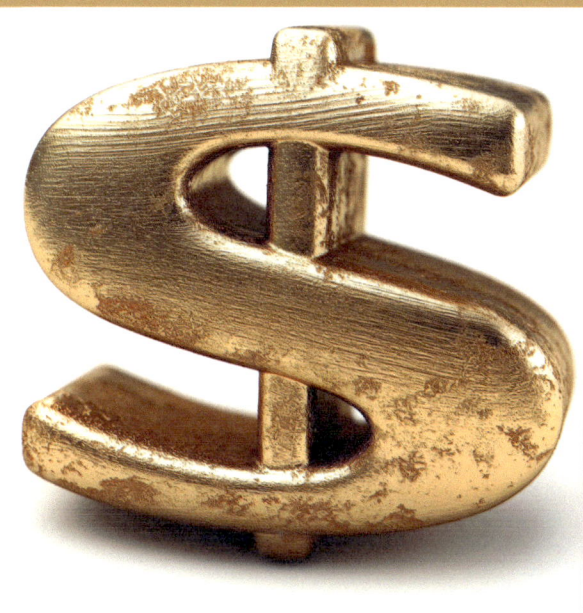
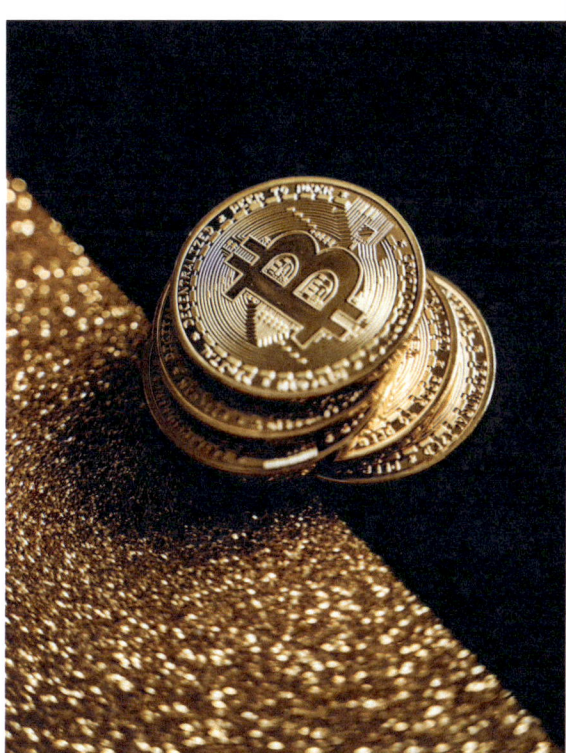

I attract wealth and abundance every day.

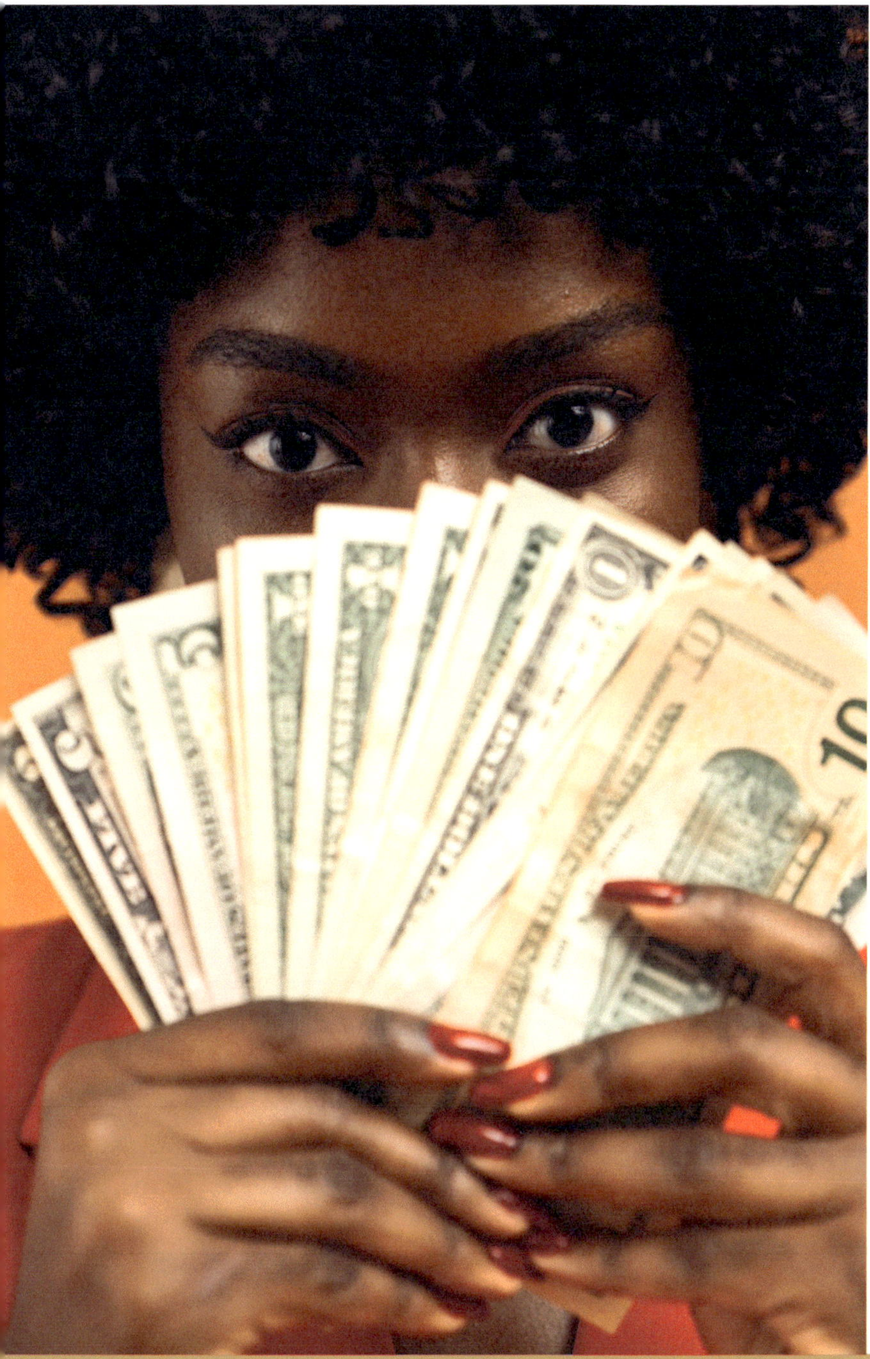

Debt Management & Financial Freedom

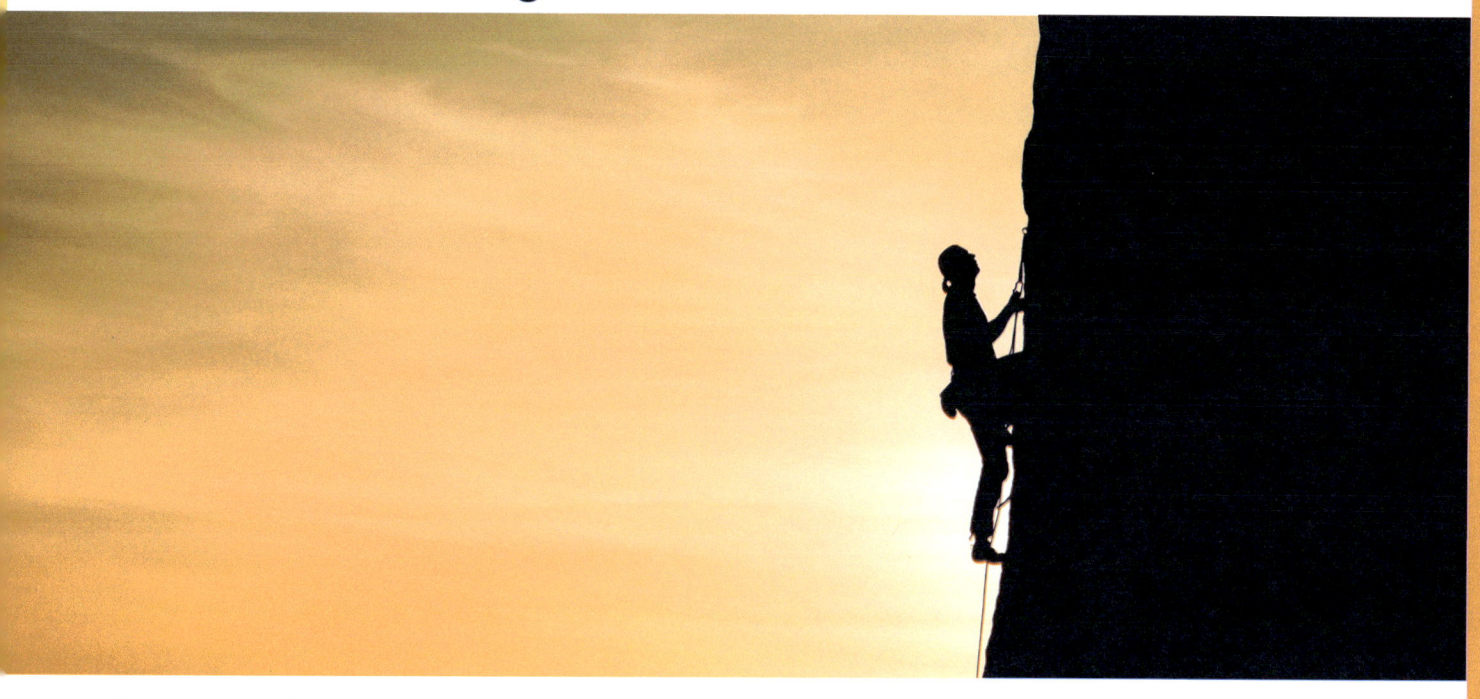

Budgeting and Saving to manage and reduce debt.

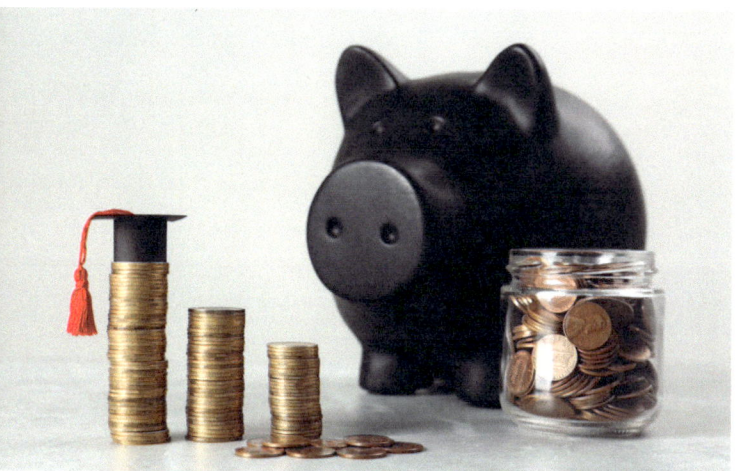
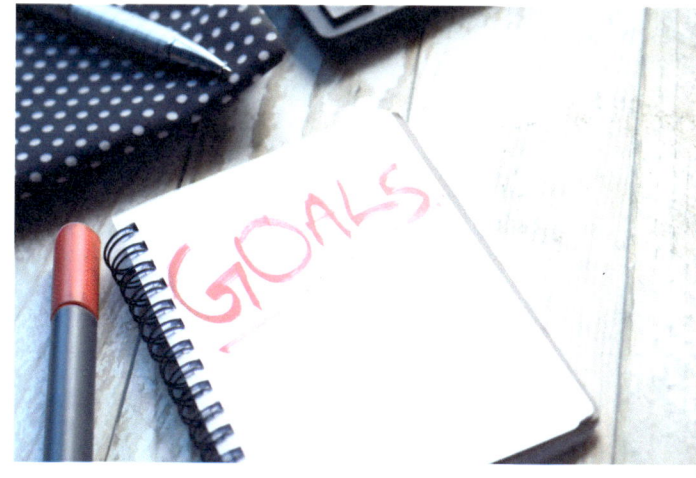

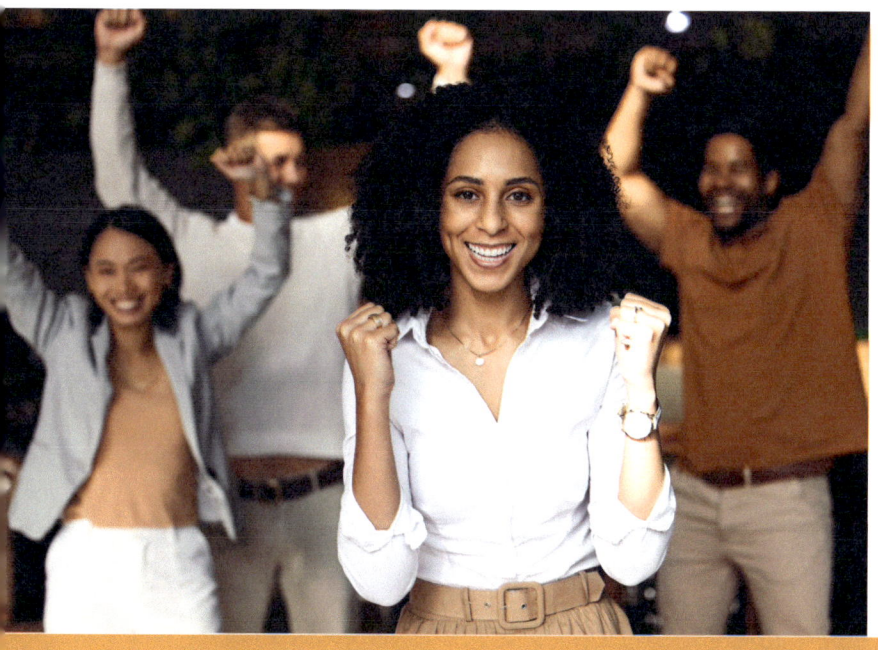

I am achieving financial freedom.

Entrepreneur

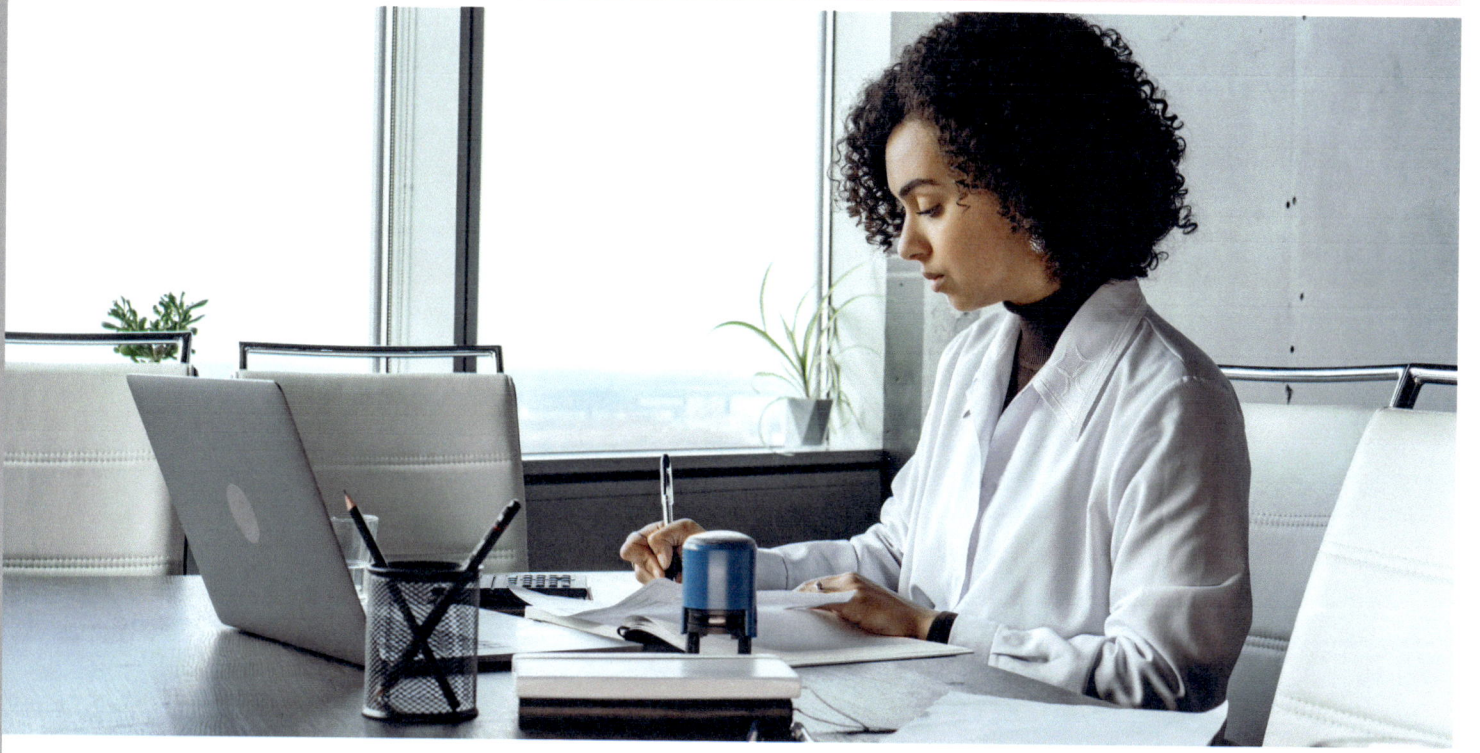

Side Hustle Ideas

Blogging and Content Creation

Self Published Authors

Natural Hair Care and Beauty Products

Online Coaching and Mentoring

Event Planning and Coordination

Fashion and Accessory Design

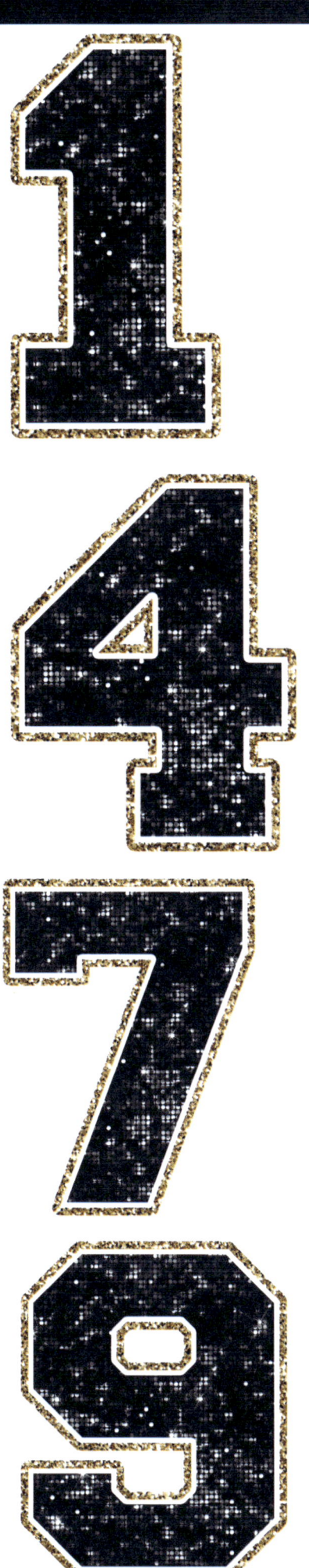
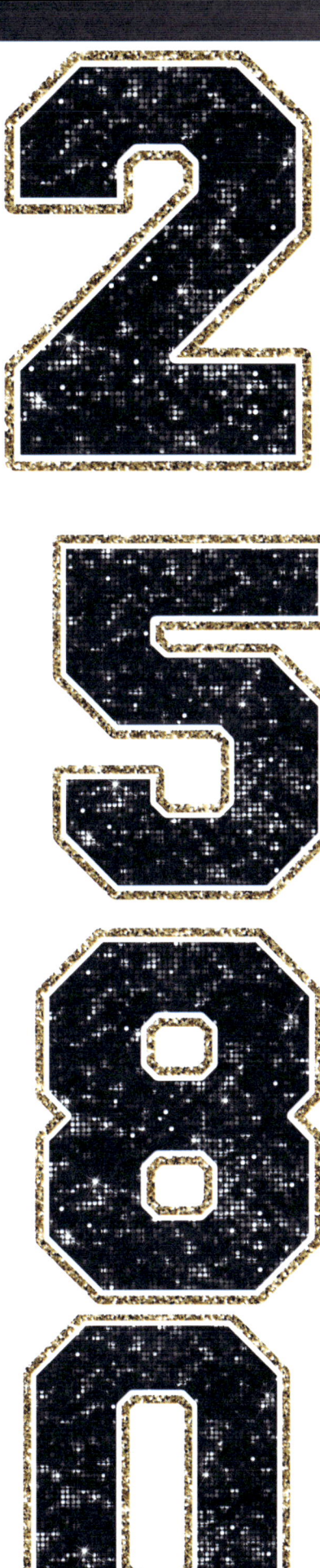
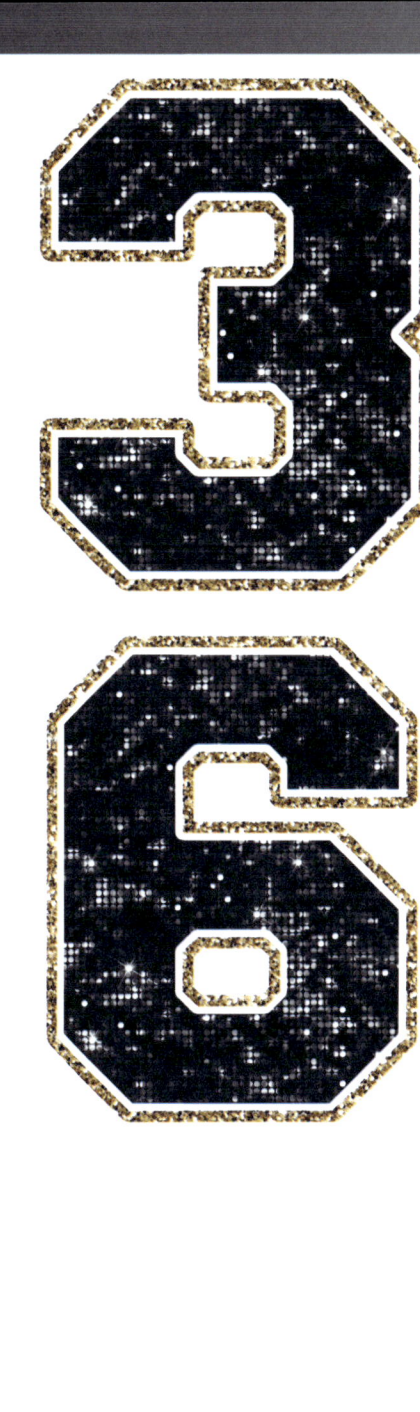

A B C D
E F G H
I J K L
M N O P
Q R S T
U V W X
Y Z

Manifestation Checks

000

Date _____

Pay To The Order Of _____ $ _____

_____ Dollars

|: 000000000 |: 00000000000000||· 0000

Date _____ 20 _____

PAY TO THE ORDER OF _____ $ _____

_____ DOLLARS

Security Features Details on Back

For _____

⑆005552222⑆ ⑆005552222⑈ 0001

0001

Date _____ 20 _____

PAY TO THE ORDER OF _____ $ _____

_____ DOLLARS

Security Features Details on Back

For _____

⑆005552222⑆ ⑆005552222⑈ 0001

Made in the USA
Columbia, SC
02 March 2025

54591805R00051